—Be a—
CHANGEMASTER

Be a CHANGEMASTER

Karla Reiss

12 COACHING STRATEGIES
for Leading Professional and Personal Change

CORWIN

A SAGE Company

FOR INFORMATION:

Corwin

A SAGE Company

2455 Teller Road

Thousand Oaks, California 91320

(800) 233-9936

Fax: (800) 417-2466

www.corwin.com

SAGE Ltd.

1 Oliver's Yard

55 City Road

London EC1Y 1SP

United Kingdom

SAGE India Pvt. Ltd.

B 1/I 1 Mohan Cooperative Industrial Area

Mathura Road, New Delhi 110 044

India

SAGE Asia-Pacific Pte. Ltd.

33 Pekin Street #02-01

Far East Square

Singapore 048763

Acquisitions Editor: Arnis Burvikovs

Associate Editor: Desirée A. Bartlett

Editorial Assistant: Kimberly Greenberg

Production Editor: Cassandra Margaret Seibel

Copy Editor: Diane J. DiMura

Typesetter: C&M Digitals (P) Ltd.

Proofreader: Jennifer Gritt

Indexer: Joan Shapiro

Cover Designer: Rose Storey

Permissions Editor: Karen Ehrmann

Copyright © 2012 by Karla Reiss

Printed in the United States of America.

Library of Congress Cataloging-in-Publication Data

Reiss, Karla.

Be a changemaster : 12 coaching strategies for leading professional and personal change / Karla Reiss.

p. cm.
Includes bibliographical references and index.

ISBN 978-1-4129-9745-4 (pbk.)

1. School personnel management. 2. Educational leadership. 3. Organizational change. 4. Self-actualization (Psychology) I. Title.

LB2831.5.R45 2012
371.2'01—dc23   2011043024

This book is printed on acid-free paper.

12 13 14 15 16 10 9 8 7 6 5 4 3 2 1

Contents

Additional materials and resources related to
Be a CHANGEMASTER: 12 Coaching Strategies for Leading Professional and Personal Change can be found at www.corwin.com/changemaster.

Preface

Challenges are what make life interesting; overcoming them is what makes life meaningful.

Joshua J. Marine

The news about change efforts is usually grim. Reports indicate up to 75 percent of organizational change efforts fail, meaning only about 25 percent are successful! According to Julia Ross (2000) in her book *The Diet Cure*, there is only a 2 percent long-term success rate of dieting. It has become common knowledge that change is hard; no one likes change and people will resist it. It has even become acceptable to think this way. Whether you are reading this book as a leader responsible for guiding your organization to a thriving future, or an individual hoping to make a personal change, these data bits can be downright depressing.

Every leader must be competent to lead every individual to change. Leaders at all levels in the organization need specific skills and a deep understanding of how to guide people and groups toward the needed changes so the organization survives and thrives. Every leader dreaming, wishing, and hoping to make a lasting change needs a new mind-set and a concrete set of skills that foster successful change.

We can no longer accept the rate of failure of change efforts. It is too costly. I know of no organization that has 75 percent of their time and financial resources to waste in change efforts that result in a great plan sitting on a shelf creating little to no change. I know of no person who doesn't have the best intention for his or her goal to finally happen. The future and success of your organization and your career, depends on having the know-how, confidence, competence, and courage to lead others to transform their thoughts, beliefs, behaviors, and actions to achieve their desired change.

When I searched Amazon.com for books on "change" I found 116,275. When I refined the search to "change management" I found 13,446 books. The key words *leading change* highlighted 703 books and *personal change*—3,736 books, with some overlap among categories. Professional and personal development are big and booming industries. According to a 2009 Marketdata Enterprises report, the self-improvement market in the United States was worth $10.5 billion. Professional coaching was growing at a rate of 6.2 percent per year. Leaders and individuals are hungry for the best advice and how-to tips to overcome the challenges of creating change in their professional and personal lives. Coaching is considered a must-have skill for today's leaders.

When people start out on a change path, it often feels like they are fighting an uphill battle, going against the grain and swimming upstream. With so much going against them it can be easy to give up before beginning—or soon afterward. That's what usually happens.

You don't have to join in the chorus and sing that same old song that "change is hard; no one likes change." Change does not have to be seen that way, nor does it have to be feared.

I would like every reader to adopt a new mind-set that change can be easy. OK, maybe not easy as pie but certainly easier, achievable, and surely within your reach. In this book, I will show you how you can easily implement twelve specific strategies and become a CHANGEMASTER!

If you have ever been frustrated by leading a change effort, people who resist it, or making a personal change in your life, I hope you will find salvation and hope by delving into the twelve strategies to achieve lasting change. You can become a CHANGEMASTER by studying, learning, and thinking about how each of them are crucial to making successful change.

Purpose

In this book, I offer you the gift of fresh thinking about change to ease your work and ease the process of creating lasting change—at last! If you are a leader of people and responsible for organizational change, it is my wish and hope that this book equips you with practical strategies for managing resistance to change.

I have a long-held belief in the importance of leaders adopting a "coaching style" of leadership and internalize the coaching process to reach more people in more cost-effective ways. You do not have to become a fully certified and credentialed coach, which can be a lengthy and costly process. You can develop the insight and knowledge to learn and apply the strategies that professionally trained coaches use.

This book is intended to be a practical resource for helping organizational leaders and individuals rethink the challenge of change and develop positive strategies to achieve it. Too many change initiatives fail because we don't often know how to lead successful change. Failed efforts are very costly to the goals and momentum of the organization, costly in terms of wasted energy, dollars, and intention. We might know how to create change in theory, however, change is an individual process for each person and it is important for leaders to finally know how to master change.

Readers will discover how to partner with people to overcome resistance to change. I hope this book inspires leaders to consider how coaching should be considered and adopted as a systemic change strategy. It is different from other books about change, which are typically theoretical. This book provides practical strategies and tips that will enable you to banish old, ineffective thinking about change and adopt a "change can be easy" mind-set. It is an "encyclopedia of change."

The content and CHANGEMASTER strategies in the chapters that follow are based on professional coaching strategies versus change management theory common to other books about change. This book differs in that it will help leaders adopt a coaching style of leadership without specific coach training. While this is not a book filled with descriptions of various research projects, it is based on research about how we can achieve successful change that is incorporated into the work of professional coaches. It will provide specific hands-on, easily doable strategies and tools you can implement immediately with staff, teams, and your entire organization.

The body of knowledge this book is based on is derived from the field of professional coaching, and from research on brain function, not from years of formal research into the change process. I will share with you what I have learned about people and change from the world and work of professional coaching. For coaching is how we support people to create change, one person at a time. Coaching is a proven process for creating change in individuals and entire organizations.

Who Should Read This Book

If you are one of the people who has bought into the concept that change is hard, this book is for you. This book will serve many audiences. It is designed to be useful for both individuals who wish to make personal change in their lives, and organizational leaders who are responsible for managing a change effort. If you are a superintendent, CEO, executive director, department manager, team leader, or any leader of people who are responsible for achieving challenging goals, you will find this book practical and useful. University professors and teachers of courses that focus on leadership, organizational development coaching programs can use this book as a unique and helpful text.

Background

I don't know about you, but I became tired of listening to people moan and groan about how hard change is. Individuals who want to change something in their life and never quite achieve their goal often give up. Leaders who claim staff won't change, no one likes change, change is impossible, or people will resist often do not know what to do when resistance arises.

Allow me to shake up your thinking about change. I decided to write this book to change your mind-set about change. Change can be easy and in the chapters following are a dozen specific things you can do to discover just how easy it can be.

The twelve strategies described in this book came to me late one night while stranded overnight in an airport. There were no hotels available, and I had no choice but to stay awake all night and wait for my early morning flight. I had just come from a speaking engagement at a high school. Many high school staff members are said to be very traditional and resisting change. As I left this event, I thought about ways to help them adopt new ways to think about change in a positive "I can do it" way.

So there I was at midnight in the Chicago airport with my need to stay awake and my thoughts about how to help people consider new ways to think about change. That is when the idea for this book hit me in the form of an acronym: CHANGEMASTER—created to help leaders and individuals remember what is needed to create change and to communicate how easy change can be. I was energized by the idea. It helped me stay awake all night as I feverishly created the beginning of what is now this book. I hope it serves to support you in making important changes, work with people who resist change, and help your challenging goals become reality. Most of all, I hope it helps you rethink change; discover that change can be easy and become a master of change!

How to Use This Book

This book is organized into twelve strategies that evolved from my work with school leaders and individuals over the past ten years as a professional coach. All twelve strategies are derived from the coaching field, and represent what coaches do with individual clients, groups or entire organizations, to cultivate successful change. The acronym CHANGEMASTER is meant to assist readers with a simple-to-remember format that change can be easy. This is a flexible book. The twelve strategies can be applied to any or all change efforts— changes for the organization, teams, individuals, or the leader. They can be applied to personal changes or professional ones. I recommend before you implement the ideas in this chapter that you read the entire book so you can grasp all twelve strategies for change. Get to know what is meant by each one, and practice with people. You can easily apply the same strategies in this book to groups that you apply to individuals.

Once you become familiar with the strategies in the following chapters, feel free to try any or all of them. Although each one is important to achieving your desired change, there is no particular order you must follow. Choose one and get going. Choose the one that either resonates with you the most, or the one where you think people are stuck.

Each chapter contains success stories that demonstrate how the strategies described in this book have led to transformational change. Readers will also find one or more useful tools to help them implement the strategies today and tips for success. You can try the strategies and the tools yourself before introducing them to your staff, if you wish, or you can jump right in and be a CHANGEMASTER.

Each contributor who shared a success story using these strategies is a professional coach with no less than sixty hours of training. To respect the confidential nature of coaching, their names, locations and organizations have been changed, unless otherwise indicated.

Universal Application

The strategies in this book are different from those you would typically find in a leadership book. They encompass the whole person. They include mental (thoughts), physical (action), emotional (feelings), and spiritual (meaningful purpose) attributes. While this book has a bias toward leadership and organizational change, every strategy is equally useful for you as an individual in achieving any change. Want to launch a business, achieve your ideal goal weight, retire to Tahiti, or change careers? Feel free to use the tools and strategies to stop thinking you can't and start getting your plan in motion.

Many of the examples used in the chapters that follow are about school systems. As a former educator, I am passionate about fostering change in such challenging organizations. The concepts, tools, and strategies are practical and useful for nonprofit organizations, government agencies, and businesses of any size, too. You can easily apply them in any setting.

Three Main Reasons to Buy This Book

- To provide leaders and individuals with practical, doable coaching strategies they can apply today to create successful change
- To adopt a new, positive mind-set that change can be easy and within your reach
- To provide insight, skills, and understanding of a coaching style of leadership

Special Features

- Useful tools you can use for planning and professional development
- Inspiring quotes
- Tips for success

You can start adopting a coaching style of leadership today. Doing so will offer understanding about how change is truly and finally made. You will learn how to foster change in others by using the twelve strategies in this book. They are all coaching strategies. Coaching is very much an inside-out process. Internally changing how we think, what we believe, and what we do leads to external change in behavior, action, and results.

Enjoy the (easier) journey . . .

Acknowledgments

I never aspired to be, or thought of myself as, a writer. For some people, writing is their life's work. For me, it evolved and became a means for communicating something important that I wanted to share with others. I wanted to inspire people and provide hope for achieving successful and lasting change.

This book would never have made it past the thought stage if it were not for the kind nudging by senior editor at Corwin, Arnis Burvikovs. Many thanks to Cassandra Seibel, project editor; Desirée Bartlett, associate editor; and Kimberly Greenberg, editorial assistant, for your collective guidance. Everyone at Corwin has been a tremendous pleasure to work with. I am very grateful for the Corwin editorial board who believes in my work and its value, and I am proud to be among the fine company of Corwin authors.

There are dozens of individuals and former clients whom I have not only learned so much from but whose courage, persistence and amazing results propel me to continue this work. I would like to thank the professional coaches (and their clients) who shared their success stories with me. Among them are Charles Elbot, Denver Public Schools, and Lindsley Silagi, Santa Teresa, New Mexico. Others who shared stories prefer to remain anonymous. I thank you, too. To protect confidentiality, I cannot mention all the names of the clients who bravely embraced coaching and tackled their goals. If you are a former client or student of our Powerful Coaching for Powerful Results™ program, please know how grateful I am for your presence, your enthusiasm, and your commitment to learn this valuable process and bring it to others.

As our work and training has grown, I want to thank the many professional coaches who have partnered with me to facilitate our training programs. Thank you for sharing your expertise, your time, and passion for coaching. Among them are Denny Balish, Carla Geddes,

Elaine Gnessin, Janice McDermott, Kathy Quinn, Sheldon Romer, Chuck Schroeder, Lindsley Silagi, and Steve Silverman and our Canadian coaches: Beryl Allport, Robert Carscadden, Ann Fogolin, Marie-Claude Lapalme, and Debra Forman. The list continues as we expand.

Heartfelt thanks to my husband Ed who has patiently and lovingly left me alone so I can carve out the time and space I needed to write this book. Thank you for reading every word and for everything you do to enable me to pursue my life's work.

My family members have been wonderful cheerleaders. To my mom, Dobbie, my children Michael and Emily, and my extended family, Matt, Bridget, Shanna, and Michelle, thank you for your encouragement and being a meaningful part of my life!

Publisher's Acknowledgments

Corwin would like to thank the following individuals for taking the time to provide their editorial insight:

Darlene K. Castelli, Reading Specialist, Literacy Coach, and Literacy Coordinator
Clayton High School
Clayton, MO

Mary Ann Hartwick, Principal
Litchfield Elementary School
Litchfield Park, AZ

Kay Kuenzl-Stenerson, Literacy Coach
Merrill Middle School
Oshkosh, WI

Alice Manus, Assistant Principal of Academics: Curriculum, Instruction, Guidance, and Counseling
Soldan International Studies High School
St. Louis, MO

Kay Teehan, Technology Resource Specialist
School Technology Services
Polk County Schools
Lakeland, FL

About the Author

**Karla Reiss** is the award-winning author of *Leadership Coaching for Educators: Bringing Out the Best in School Administrators*. She founded The Change Place, LLC, a coaching and consulting firm dedicated to the continuous improvement of individuals, teams, and organizations, in 2002 after 30 years in education, publishing, and sales. She and her team of certified coaches offer several levels of coaching training programs to leaders of school systems, government and non-profit organizations, businesses, and individuals who wish to learn a coaching style of leadership, including *Powerful Coaching for Powerful Results*™ certification program, *CKEY: Coaching Kids, Empowering Youth*™, and various related programs. The Change Place, LLC also provides executive and leadership coaching services, workplace and leadership assessments, and products that support others to lead professional and personal change. She is also a frequent speaker at national, state, and local conferences.

As a school administrator, Reiss worked with more than 50 school districts in a variety of school improvement roles, the majority as coordinator of professional development at Western Suffolk (NY) Board of Cooperative Education Services. She has conducted numerous professional development programs and school improvement opportunities for K–12 staff and district leaders. She is certified in strategic planning and served on the New York State Education Department's statewide steering committee for Comprehensive District Education Planning. She was president of New York State Staff Development Council and served on the Executive Board of the Long Island Association for Curriculum and Staff Development.

Karla Reiss is a graduate from the Institute of Professional Excellence in Coaching in 2002 and received additional coach training at the College of Executive Coaching. She holds a bachelor of science degree, a master's degree in special education, and a professional diploma in school district administration. Her professional and personal inspiration and transition into the world of coaching was a result of the invitation to participate in Oxygen TV's program, *The Life Makeover Project* in 2002. She has applied all of the coaching techniques and strategies described in this book to her own life and now helps others courageously transition their lives, leadership style, and organizations to fulfill their goals, hopes, and dreams.

She lives the life of her dreams in Boulder, Colorado. Reiss can be reached at www.thechangeplace.com or changemaven@thechange place.com.

Introduction

When we are no longer able to change a situation, we are challenged to change ourselves.

Victor Frankl, Holocaust survivor

Last year I was contacted by the Upper Canada District School Board to help Learning Resource Coaches and other staff and district leaders develop their coaching skills. A few months later, Tim Mills, system principal, noticed some initial and immediate changes: better communication among the leadership team and reduced stress from letting go of the (former) need to know the answers; people were asking better questions and listening at a deeper level. The district is the broadest implementation of professional coaching skills I know of. Staff members used the strategies described in this book after learning how to develop a coaching mind-set and implementing professional coaching skills.

The district was under pressure to change, sparked by declining enrollment and a lofty goal of 90 percent graduation rate for their 27,000 thousand students in eighty-four buildings across an eight thousand square mile area. Over two hundred staff members were trained. Some used coaching skills with other staff, leaders, and some directly with students. Although everyone was experienced and knowledgeable in their respective subject areas, they sought to be more effective developing professional relationships with colleagues. They wanted to feel welcome into the classrooms of their peers and know how to engage in deeper conversations about learning and improving student achievement.

It has become crystal clear that individuals and leaders hunger for ways to manage change and the high levels of frustrating resistance that accompanies it. Today's leaders need to implement radical changes and develop the know-how for it to happen. There is great urgency to "get change right." Our education systems, nonprofit organizations, government agencies, and businesses, large or small, are out of time and resources to study the research, or if they have already done so and not successfully applied the learning, this book can be considered a quick-start guide to mastering change.

Up to 20 percent of any size group will strongly resist change, 20 percent will be enthusiastic and the remaining 60 percent will agree to engage in a change effort. The diagram below shows that 60 to 80 percent (all of the resistors plus the middle-of-the-roaders) will require support and leadership intervention to actively and positively engage in a change effort. The twelve CHANGEMASTER strategies will help with specific methods for dealing with the most resistant 20 percent and the cautious 60 percent (Rogers, 2003).

20% Supportive and positive toward change. *Ready to go.*	60% On the fence—need leadership and coaching to guide toward change. *Will proceed with caution.*	20% Negative toward change. The naysayers. *Will resist.*

The Coaching–Change Connection: The Inside-Out Approach

Until ten years ago, I didn't know how to create change. I bought into the common woe-is-me attitude, frustration, and belief that change is hard. Change felt like a battle and every step a fight. That was before I was introduced to coaching. It was then that I developed the insight, know-how, skills, and techniques that helped me and my eventual clients shift from "Change is hard" to "Change is easy." Through coaching, I learned that change is an individual journey for each person. Leaders must start to deal with people individually and adopt a coaching style of leadership that enables change to occur.

For years, I felt challenged in several areas of my life, both professional and personal. I sought ways to help leaders be more effective at implementing change. I wanted to be a better leader but didn't know quite how to go about it, and I wanted to make some changes in my personal life to attain greater meaning and happiness. I found the majority of books and training programs too theoretical to translate into practical things I could do. I tried various techniques, read every leadership and self-help book I could find, joined professional organizations, and continued my learning.

Then in 2001 I discovered coaching. Through both being a coaching client and becoming a certified coach, I became convinced that coaching is the process every leader needs to know about and know how to do if they want to create meaningful and lasting change. Coaching is the change process and leaders everywhere need to master the skills and strategies coaches use in order to affect change in their organizations.

Coaching is a strategy, set of skills, tools, and techniques for creating meaningful and lasting change. It is important for readers to know that the strategies in this book form the heart of what seasoned coaches do with clients. You don't have to become a professional coach to create successful change with others (although it would help). You can and will overcome resistance to change by using the strategies that follow.

I believe the main reason change has been challenging for leaders is the lack of common knowledge and skill about coaching skills and the coaching process. Typically, the amount of time and money to become skilled in coaching prevents most people or enough people from bringing it successfully within an organization. Or many people use the term *coaching* with little or no insight or training into how the work of a coach is defined and implemented. Every leader needs to know how to coach. It should be taught in every leadership preparation program.

Coaching works. Coaching is effective because it is the change process. So let's disperse the knowledge throughout and within organizations and enable this powerful process to spread. In my book, *Leadership Coaching for Educators* (2007), I introduced educators to the International Coach Federation's Professional Coaching Core Competencies. They are the standards for the coaching profession and define what should be taught to coaches. This book takes the next step by integrating them with the twelve CHANGEMASTER strategies.

Coaching is still emerging as a profession. Yet we can all learn, understand, and act with a coaching mind-set and a coaching skill set whether or not we pursue it as a profession. The twelve strategies in this book are the same strategies used by professional coaches. Use them often and discover how to lead others to change.

Let's start by defining coaching. The dictionary defines *coach* as a vehicle "used to take people on a journey." I especially like this term because a leader with a coaching approach is surely leading people on a journey, from their current state to a transformed future.

The International Coach Federation professional coach definition is this:

> *Coaching is an ongoing relationship which focuses on client taking action toward the realization of their visions, goals or desires.*

> *Coaching uses a process of inquiry and personal discovery to build the client's level of awareness and responsibility and provides the client with structure, support and feedback.*

> *The coaching process helps clients define and achieve professional and personal goals faster and with more ease than would be possible otherwise.*

The International Association of Coaching defines it this way:

> *Coaching is a transformative process for personal and professional awareness, discovery and growth.*

While coaching focuses on external goals, these goals are often achieved by focusing on the inner self. Change efforts have long focused on mental and physical processes—what we want to do, what it will cost, and what resources are needed. Those emerge from our logical-thinking, left, rational brain. Those left-brained thoughts often talk you or others, *out* of the change. They will tell you why it can't happen and why change is too hard, too costly, or impossible to achieve.

For change to be effective and lasting, it must address a combination of the mental, physical, emotional, and spiritual. Leaders must become skilled in leading from the heart and touching the right brain, where hopes and dreams lie. Coaching is a holistic process, and a coaching approach addresses the head, heart, and soul. When people learn to coach, they learn to affect inside-out change, helping them observe their beliefs, thoughts, behavior, and action; noticing their driving values; and seeing new possibilities in a safe, trusting relationship.

Coaching has evolved from several fields, including the following:

- Neuroscience
- Positive psychology
- Sports psychology

- Solution-focused psychology
- Adult learning
- Metaphysics
- Personal development
- Studies of human potential

One of the most astounding findings derived from the above fields is that we always own the ability to choose. Contrary to what most people think, they can choose what they think, believe, and do, the same way they choose what to wear. Coaching supports change efforts by skillfully listening and questioning thoughts and beliefs while helping people see that they can choose differently. No longer does the old excuse "I can't help it" work. A person *can* help it. A person *can* change it. We all can change when we choose to.

What this means for anyone confronting a change is that by adopting a coaching approach and the strategies in this book, you can eradicate the excuses that have stood in the way of change. You can lead and guide others to make successful change.

A Coaching Approach

There is a dramatic and meaningful shift in the nature of conversations from everyday talk to skilled conversations that promote introspection, self-discovery, action, and commitments. Skilled leaders with a coaching approach listen more deeply. They ask more powerful, open, discovery-type questions. They are no longer the provider of answers; instead, they become partners in exploring and developing possibilities, guiding others to find solutions. Coaching supports empowerment in the workplace.

The city of Richmond's vision was to be the most appealing, livable, and well-managed community in the country. They introduced coaching as a strategy to develop leadership skills with their management team. According to Human Resources Manager Rae Williamson, "Richmond trained more than 140 managers. We've seen a different culture emerging; one that is more collaborative, where employees step forward with ideas and contributions. Our people believe they are being heard" (Williamson quoted in Smith, 2009). "Coaching supports collaboration. Managers are starting to realize the value of coaching" (Rush quoted in Smith, 2009).

What Comprises a Coaching Style of Leadership?

A coaching style of leadership is very different from a traditional style. Traditional leadership has been top-down in which the leader has experience, knowledge, and wisdom, advising others what they should do. A coaching style of leadership is collaborative, nonjudgmental, trusting, and action oriented. It respects each individual and acknowledges professional growth as a continuum.

Traditional Leadership	*Coaching Style of Leadership*
Telling	Asking and listening
Focus on problems	Focus on solutions
Focus on staff as a whole	Focus on individuals
Voices opinions	Is nonjudgmental
Focuses on work related issues	Focuses on the whole person
Bottom-line oriented	Mission oriented
Authoritative	Collaborative
Task oriented	People oriented
Discussion oriented	Action & result oriented
Having power and control	Sharing power and control
Focus on the past	Focus on the future

Evidence of Coaching Effectiveness

Classroom only styles of learning are far less effective than when combined with coaching support as follow-up to learning. There are a growing number of inspiring reports about the effectiveness of coaching.

In the December 2006 issue of *Training and Development,* corporate training expenditures were estimated to have reached $109.25 billion. In most cases, much of these training dollars failed to deliver significant impact.

The 2011 Report on Professional and Management Development Training (Anything Research, 2011) looked at a variety of coaching initiatives. Most studied the result of executive coaching of leaders by an external, professional coach. The reported results are as follows:

- Executive coaching at Booz Allen Hamilton delivered $7.90 return on investment.
- Another survey by Manchester, Inc. of 140 companies suggested the average return was 5 times the initial investment.
- A telecommunications company received 529 percent return on investment along with intangible benefits.
- Kodak's coaching program for 1,000 employees delivered double digit increases in employee productivity (Professional and Management Training, n.d.).

Other measurable results from organizational coaching were reported by International Personnel Management Association include improvement in these areas:

- Productivity   53 percent
- Quality   48 percent
- Customer service   39 percent
- Teamwork   67 percent
- Job satisfaction   61 percent
- Working relationships   77 percent
  with direct reports   (Hoagland-Smith, 2006)

In April 2009, the International Coach Federation published the Global Coaching Client Study of 2,165 coaching clients from 64 countries participated from September to November 2008. Respondents were asked to rate the areas they experienced a positive impact from being coached:

- Self-esteem/self-confidence   80 percent
- Relationships   73 percent
- Communication skills   72 percent
- Interpersonal skills   71 percent
- Work performance   70 percent
- Work/life balance   67 percent
- Career opportunities   62 percent
- Personal organization   61 percent
- Business management   61 percent
- Team effectiveness   57 percent
- Corporate culture   51 percent

These positive results are staggering and inspiring. Everyone with an interest in continuous improvement and professional growth can learn to coach others. It is my hope and meaningful purpose that all leaders gain coaching know-how and help others achieve these results. Doing so will most certainly enhance your change efforts. I urge all leaders to adopt a coaching approach style of leadership and encourage you to use the coaching strategies in this book with others.

The Challenge of Change

It is easy to understand why the prevalent mode of thinking that change is hard is derived from research on change, since the majority of restructuring or change efforts fail. No wonder the buzz about leading change is that it is difficult to accomplish.

Change has a bad rap. Because the majority of organizational and personal change efforts are unsuccessful, there is even more urgency for leaders to discover the keys to success. You do not have to buy in to thinking it will always be this way.

Organizations don't change; people do. Organizational change efforts don't fail because of a lack of smarts or resources or the just-right strategies. They fail because successful change is about people, and leaders need to understand how to coach people, one at a time.

Successful change is an individual process. Leaders need to view change in terms of what each person needs. One will either move toward the change, resist it, or stagnate. Leaders need to individualize the change process by tapping in to the hearts, minds, and souls of each person. They need to know how each person views the goal or change from an emotional, spiritual, and mental perspective. Leaders need to know and understand what the person is thinking, believing. They need to develop relationships based on trust so inner thoughts can comfortably emerge.

We have evolved to a place where we know that one charismatic leader cannot make a sustainable difference. It is essential to build capacity for creating lasting change; establishing habits of mind that create a positive culture, where personal and professional growth are honored.

Judith Harvey, former superintendent, Maine

Professional coaching has skyrocketed in recent years. The reason is the effectiveness of this strategy in creating change. That is what coaching is all about—change! The practice of coaching in many organizations has focused on content and skill development, when in reality coaching focuses on the inner thoughts and beliefs that lead to or inhibit action toward a goal. A skilled coach is an expert in change, changing thoughts, minds, actions, and results. Leaders will adopt a "coaching style of leadership" when they use the twelve CHANGEMASTER strategies.

Become a CHANGEMASTER

Skilled coaches specialize in creating change in people. Achieving successful change is not about content knowledge, nor is it focused on skills. Sure, sometimes we need to know how to do something and obtain new skills, but to break through the "people part" of resistance requires leaders to focus on how to work with people in ways that move them through change. It can be done!

The twelve strategies below are described in detail in each chapter that follows. They are "people" strategies. Master them and you will master successful change. They are equally applicable to use with individuals, teams, departments, and entire organizations. Use them to ease the process of personal changes for yourself and those you lead. I hope they provide hope and help for you and your organization's future.

Challenge Assumptions

Have a Higher Purpose

Awareness of Limiting Thoughts

Nix the Negatives and Naysayers

Gather a Group

Emotionally Connect to the Goal

Maintain Momentum

Ask How Can I?

See Success Smiling

Turn Talk to the Future

Expect and Welcome Discomfort

Remain Relentlessly Focused

1

Challenge Assumptions

We make assumptions, and believe we are right about the assumptions; then we defend our assumptions and try to make someone else wrong.

Don Miguel Ruiz, Author

According to the *Cambridge Advanced Learner's Dictionary*, an assumption is "something that you accept as true without question or proof." It is amazing how many of us believe in our assumptions as absolute truth. I wonder how many of you reading this have ever stopped to think about assumptions or to deeply question and examine them and the effect they have on you, your work, and your life. Until I discovered coaching, I did not either.

Everyone has assumptions. Sometimes assumptions are good. When you are in your car stopped at a stop sign, you most likely assume the car or truck approaching you from behind is going to stop. You don't think about it. You don't brace yourself, waiting to be hit. You feel safe. You probably pay no attention to your rear view mirror and are thinking about other things. Or when you turn on the water faucet, you assume water will come out. Most of the time, that is exactly what happens, unless there's a plumbing problem or water line break. You probably formed this assumption based on a lifetime of turning on the water faucet. You don't even have to think about what will happen when you need to fill your glass. Many of our assumptions are helpful to eliminate stress. They can keep us from having to think about every single thing, every time. Some things just run smoothly and do not require our attention. All good.

On the other hand, too many of our assumptions are negative, incorrect, and stagnating. During a coaching session, an aspiring principal told me she hoped to obtain a position in a nearby town. The economy was suffering and available positions were limited. The assumption she made was, "There are no jobs in this state." That thought (negative assumption) caused her to make very little effort to obtain the job, even though she truly wanted it. The negative assumption drove her behavior, which in this case was inaction.

Assumptions are thoughts that cause us to predict an outcome. They are usually based on a past experience or are old stale thoughts. We think we already know what will happen, based on the assumption we've made. Assumptions are not necessarily true; they rarely are. They are simply habitual thoughts that stifle us. If we don't stop and look at assumptions head-on, we will continue to let them rule us. Assumptions can stop us or stop progress toward our goals. They have a strong influence on what people think. They drive what people do or don't do. They can stop individuals in their tracks and entire teams from taking action and moving toward a change.

Assumptions can be our friend. They can also be the enemy of change.

If I assume a parent will be upset at our upcoming meeting, I will prepare for a confrontation. My defenses will be high, and I will be preparing for battle. On the other hand, if I release the assumption and focus my attention and preparation on a positive conversation, my words and energy will be more productive. If I assume I'm a poor speaker, I will run from opportunities that would require me to be heard. If my position requires me to speak in public, I might become physically ill at the thought, my fear would rise within me, causing me to do a poor job, just as I assumed I would.

Assumptions are not facts, but we often make the mistake of treating them as they are. If we don't change them, they become etched as a belief. When people keep them hidden, leaders might observe them as resistant. Instead of feeling frustrated, it is far better to learn to work with assumptions, help to reverse them, and create fresh thinking. This is really worth exploring to become adept at leading change efforts. As a leader, you must become more aware of what lies within the minds of people and how to work with such thoughts to create shifts in thinking and thus, action.

Assumptions are thoughts we take for granted and believe them to be true. They aren't based on facts; they are based on experiences of the past. They are fiction. Assumptions inform our decision making, and this is precisely where the problem lies. They influence the decisions we make and often cause inertia. I assume how my friend will respond to going out to an Asian restaurant with me, so I decide to say nothing, instead of asking her. I assume the supervisor will be upset that I bombed my presentation, so I become nervous to meet. Or I avoid meeting.

Assumptions are a reflection of what's going on in one's mind, where we focus our thinking. When our thoughts are voiced to someone else, we now have a great opportunity to learn the person's perception. It is precisely from that perception that change efforts can start. Suppose Alex was thinking, "I'm too old to get that job. They're looking for someone fresh out of school." As a result, Alex refrained from applying for the job, even though he really wanted it. Suppose he was a great leader who could turn that school around, but his lack of initiative created a lose-lose for him and for the district. What if instead he recognized he had unique experiences from his prior roles that could indeed be of true value? If he were willing to challenge his own assumption, he might have taken action, with confidence, and pursued his goal. Stories like this happen too often. They thwart progress and inhibit organizations from achieving their goals. They cause individuals to remain locked in their self-imposed boundaries.

Negative assumptions show up as resistance and halt progress. Usually, leaders don't know why or what is going on. Why? Because assumptions are usually kept within and not often voiced. They might be discussed in the faculty room or around the water cooler but are not often shared with our supervisors. Assumptions are usually lurking silently in the one's mind versus speaking openly about them.

> *Often unspoken, these assumptions are powerful predictors of success or subtle forces contributing to failure.*
>
> Linda Searby (2009)

Let's take the example of Alice, a teacher who is asked to participate on a new committee by her principal. Alice responds by saying *no*. Just no. She tells the principal she can't stay late to attend the meetings or gives some other excuse. In truth, those are not really the reasons for her refusal. Deep down there was something else going on—an assumption.

Let's look beneath the surface. Alice has been in the school for twelve years and been on numerous committees. Nothing ever came of them, and she began to perceive them as a waste of her precious time and energy. She lost enthusiasm, stopped being an active participant, and emotionally disengaged.

Alice formed an assumption based on a past experience. Because she had a former, negative experience, she naturally thought the same outcome would occur next time. She didn't stop and think about it. She carried on as if it were the absolute truth. So her actions, or lack of action, were based on the assumption. She didn't question it. Instead, she acted as if she already knew what the result would be, just like the water faucet. She backed off, and her principal didn't really know why.

Holding on to an assumption can cause a serious drain of energy, energy that could otherwise be used for positive purposes and supporting organizational change. Stifling thoughts create just that—no movement, no action, no results.

> *Too often we enjoy the comfort of opinion without the discomfort of thought.*
>
> John F. Kennedy

Challenge Those Assumptions

Change can be more easily mastered by Challenging Assumptions. That's right—you must be willing to confront and challenge assumptions when they arise. An assumption can be wrong. Yet it silently drives inner thoughts and actions or creates inaction. They will stay there unless the leader or coach brings them out into the open for discussion. When the leader becomes aware that assumptions might be lingering within the mind of the employee and has the courage to confront them, there is now an opportunity to break the resistance.

Leaders can make or break a goal by becoming aware of the specific assumptions one has and assuring that the "same old" won't happen again. The leader must assure the holder of the assumption that this time will be different. This time we will do it this way or that way. Different actions will lead to different results, and it is up to the leader to reassure the employees and bring them on board to the new committee. Alice might have been willing to participate in the committee if she knew her effort would lead to a meaningful result.

Anne is a creative artist, a weaver. If you've ever been to a quality art show, you know that woven art is pricey. Anne loves to create one-of-a-kind pieces for meaningful occasions. She puts a lot of love and time into each piece. Thus, the high price. Anne was hoping to make a living as a weaver. She has been working at it for years and has yet to earn a livable income.

As her coach, I came to know my client Anne well. I learned what she thinks and believes about not only her work, but about herself. She knows she tends to be an introvert. The selling side of her business intimidates her. She would be happy as a clam to spend all of her time creating. Anne developed a deep assumption that she will never make a good living as an artist. The assumption stemmed from the fact that she hadn't make a decent living (yet).

Anne's assumption was clearly based on her past experience. It caused her to comb the want ads for jobs that will supplement her income. She had no clue how to get from where she was to where she wants to be—to earn a livable income as an artist.

I met Anne at a Chamber of Commerce meeting where she talked about her work and why she was at the meeting—to look for a job. It struck me that by networking for a job, she was acting on the assumption that she'd never make it as an artist. What if she used all that energy she expended to move her art business forward instead? If she followed her passion, this time with different actions to grow her business, she just might make it.

I offered Anne a complimentary coaching session in which I challenged the assumption. I encouraged her to imagine that the assumption is wrong. OK, maybe it was true in the past. Maybe she hadn't yet been able to pay her bills by selling her pieces, but it does not have to always be that way. I told Anne she could certainly be successful if she took different actions to get to her goal.

Anne began to reflect on her goal and her actions. They weren't aligned.

Challenging Assumptions is first about helping employees notice them and realize they are holding them back. Assumptions can be changed. They can be changed by taking different action steps than in the past. Different actions yield different results, and usually increased confidence as a bonus!

Here's another example: Linda was a coaching client, a middle-level leader, who worked in a large school district that was undergoing a great deal of change. Linda had many ideas and was enthusiastic about them. Her immediate supervisor, Jean, had a high level of visible anxiety about the upcoming changes. In fact, Jean had a temper that became evident under stress. Linda learned to avoid Jean. Linda assumed Jean would fly off the handle when Linda wanted to discuss the team's goals and strategies. What did Linda do? Nothing. Linda learned to stay away from Jean. The result? Nothing.

In our coaching sessions, Linda recognized that Jean wasn't likely to change alone. Linda wanted to implement some new programs in her department and felt as though she was walking on eggshells around Jean. Linda fell into inaction. They were at a stalemate. Eventually, Linda realized it was she who had to look deeply at her assumptions and how they contributed to her stagnation, and that of the department and the school. Although it took a while for Linda to recognize that it would continue this way until she did something about it, once she realized that change began with her, she became open to examine what she could do.

Linda chose to have a conversation with Jean. She challenged her own assumption that Jean would never listen and began to take bold action. She approached Jean to schedule a meeting. Linda and I brainstormed what she could say that would be different from their conversations of the past, and would hopefully make a difference, and lead to progress. Within a few short weeks, Linda scheduled and had the meeting with Jean. Jean recognized the change in Linda and was, much to Linda's surprise, open to listening to her ideas.

> *Begin challenging your own assumptions. Your assumptions are your windows on the world. Scrub them off every once in a while or the light won't come in.*
>
> *Alan Alda*

How Assumptions Hold Us Back

Assumptions are self-limiting, first. They are negative thoughts that drive behavior. Naturally, if we buy in to our assumptions our mind is closed—closed to possibility. We are shut down and become disengaged. As a leader, you want and need everyone to be engaged, not to disengage. If an assumption is not voiced, you will never know what staff members are thinking; therefore, you cannot intervene. In a 2001 Gallup study, less than 30 percent of staff members are fully engaged at work, 55 percent are not engaged and 19 percent are actively disengaged. It gets worse over time. Among those that are disengaged, after six months, 38 percent remain engaged and after three years, only 22 percent are fully engaged at work (Loehr & Schwartz, 2003).

Imagine that everyone in your organization has let go of assumptions. What might be different? What opportunities might now exist? When you are instrumental in changing assumptions from negative to positive by changing no to yes, you will facilitate the unleashing of stuck, blocked energy and propel people to take steps and action toward the results you seek.

Attitude and outlook are one key to creating lasting change or achieving any challenging goal. You can have a boatload of education, content knowledge, and experience in the world, yet if you harbor the wrong assumptions, you stifle progress and are doomed to failure. A study of successful people by the Carnegie Institute concluded that 85 percent of success could be attributed solely to mental attitude ("Chicago Lakes Football," n.d.). A coaching approach style of leadership shows you how to work with mental attitude one person at a time.

> *My guess is that well over 80 percent of the human race goes through life without a single original thought.*
>
> H. L. Mencken

Assumptions Become Reality

The big trouble with assumptions is that they rule us and limit us. When I assume half the students in my class will not be successful, I will make far less effort to teach them than if I truly believed in their potential. Few teachers would come out and tell a colleague this, yet the thought might be there, the belief might be present and limit their efforts on the job. The students suffer. The system suffers. All students deserve a teacher who believes in their unlimited potential.

Assumptions create expectations. Expect to find a great new job and you are more likely to find one. Expect to fail and you surely will. Our outer life is truly a creation of our inner beliefs. When we give ourselves permission to take a hard look at our thoughts, assumptions, and beliefs, we set ourselves up for the breakthroughs in thinking we'll need to get to the next step, the next level, or finally make the change we want.

Thinking for Success

I recently visited the Sistine Chapel. Of course, I heard about Michelangelo's paintings since I was a small child. Finally, I had a chance to see his amazing work, the incredible height, and wondered how he possibly did this. I tried to imagine all the people who might have tried to stop him or told him he couldn't do it. What kind of person was he? What personal strength and stamina did he have to resist the naysayers and pursue his goal anyway? Most people would assume it was impossible and not attempt it. I think about the millions of people who are touched and inspired by his paintings every year and wonder—what if? What if he assumed they were right, that it was too dangerous or too difficult? What if he let himself be led by their limits and fears? What if there was no Sistine Chapel? What if you give up on your goal?

Our mind is such a powerful organ. It has been my observation and experience that leadership workshops and training programs often fall short of providing practical insight into what is needed to overcome resistance. It takes a great deal of courage and personal stamina to be willing to banish your own assumptions. As a leader, it takes new insights into why people resist and most importantly, how to work with that resistance with each person.

Identify an assumption you hold or heard:

_____

_____

_____

Questions to ask yourself:

What if it was untrue?

What would happen if you let go of it?

_____

_____

_____

> Assumptions are the termites of relationships.
>
> Henry Winkler

All change starts with opening our eyes and mind. The problem with assumptions is that we allow them to become etched in our belief system. Once they are embedded and lurking in our mind as truth, we shut down and allow them to take over. They are truly damaging, not in the same way as deep psychological problems. They are immobilizing, negative thoughts that need to dissolve so the mind is wide open to reconsider its thoughts.

Change Your Thoughts at Any Time

I am a strong believer that the thoughts locked in our inner mind are the single most critical factor in causing resistance to change or in achieving personal or organizational goals. Leadership programs need to consider how they will teach leaders techniques and skills for unlocking and changing negative thoughts into positive ones. They need to offer skill building and a coaching approach to achieving change from the inside out.

One's thoughts do not have to be permanent. I've heard so many people ruminate on age-old thoughts that they believe are so embedded in their bones that they don't realize they can be changed. We can change our thoughts at any time. The thoughts we had yesterday don't have to be the thoughts we have today or tomorrow. We can simply change them. Everyone can do this.

Leaders need to develop the skills to support and help people change their thinking. We can't magically change other people. They have to do the work. They have to be willing. Leaders can acquire the know-how to support it. You don't have to throw up your hands in frustration that nothing can be done. Changing thinking requires a willingness to observe, reflect, and consider new possibilities.

Leaders also need to know how to guide others to change their inner thoughts.

Here's a guiding thought—what you think about, you create more of. The more you think about something, the bigger it gets. So if we dwell on our assumptions, our outer actions will reflect them. What we think about expands. Let's work with this thought. Changing thoughts is a matter of creating new ones to replace the old ones. We want to intentionally shift from negative to positive, from old to new, from thoughts that stagnate to thoughts that empower. We do this by mentally creating a new thought instead. (See Chapter 3: Awareness of Limiting Thoughts.)

How to Challenge and Banish Assumptions

A coaching approach style of leadership means helping others notice when assumptions arise and how they can negatively impact an outcome. One of the most powerful things leaders can do is ask challenging questions that inspire discovery, new insights, and new action. You can ask powerful and probing questions that challenge an assumption when you hear one. Those questions would help people think about their presuppositions and unquestioned beliefs. It is critical that leaders of schools and other organizations achieve the insight and know-how to uncover, challenge, and banish assumptions. Challenging Assumptions requires awareness and an open mind.

Challenging and letting go of assumptions begins with a willingness to become more reflective, become willing to let go of our "rightness," and revisit the thoughts we are holding on to. Examining your own thoughts and beliefs is an act of courage. Cracking open a closed mind takes insight, willingness, skill, and practice.

Scientific research is based on proving or disproving an assumption. Everyone is familiar with that process and agrees it is useful. It teaches us to question why something happens or prove otherwise. In science, we don't believe assumptions until the experiment proves the truth. When we Challenge an Assumption based on a thought we have, we can help people prove or disprove their thoughts.

Sharing personal thoughts with another can feel risky. As a leader of change, are you willing to get beneath the surface and learn what one thinks? When someone reveals a negative assumption, what will you do with this new information? How will you respond? How might you respond if you are trying to lead someone to an outcome?

Some guiding principles that will help you Challenge Assumptions are to adopt a sense of curiosity and wonder. Strive to gain a deeper understanding of why one thinks a certain way, from a discovery perspective, not from a judgmental one. Be willing to challenge the status quo and help others unlock old thoughts and courageously open their mind to new possibilities. Other helpful concepts are to unleash creative thinking. Seek ways and opportunities to encourage relaxation and help others find time to daydream, to ponder. Our best ideas emerge when we are in a relaxed state.

Here are some sample comments and questions you can use to challenge and banish assumptions:

- I notice you are assuming that . . .
- Where might that assumption come from?

- How did you arrive at that assumption?
- What if that assumption was untrue?
- What might happen if you chose a different action or thought?
- How can you verify or disprove that assumption as truth?

Same Action $\rightarrow$ **Same Results**

or

Different Action $\rightarrow$ **Different Results**

Tips for Success

For people new to the coaching strategies in this book, it can feel uncomfortable to engage in the type of dialogue that "goes inside" one's thoughts and mind, at first. Feel free to practice these strategies in advance with someone you are comfortable with. In addition, here are some tips to help you be successful:

- Suspend all judgment. You will be more successful with a non-judgmental approach. Suspending judgment can be difficult. It is an opportunity for you to let go and be open to receive the conversation that will follow.
- Build trusting relationships. Success in challenging assumptions will depend on the quality of the relationship between the people involved. The relationship needs to be based on openness, honesty, and trust.
- Listen deeply for assumptions.
- Tell the person when you hear an assumption. By doing so, you are creating awareness.

  "I hear an assumption that you think we will waste money on that project."

- Ask open-ended questions that challenge current thinking. Open-ended questions get to the heart of one's thoughts and cause them to question assumption and reconsider them.

  "What led you to that conclusion?"

  "Why do you think it will happen that way?"

  "What if you tried another approach?"

  "What makes you think that?"

- Help people rethink the issue. Help them envision possibilities and different outcomes.

  "We will research best practices before we invest."

- Help them create new and different actions to assure yielding different results

  "What can you do differently?"

  "What can you do that you haven't done before?"

> What the caterpillar calls the end of the world the master calls a butterfly.
>
> Richard Bach

Summary

Achieving successful change can be more easily accomplished by paying attention to assumptions. Keep in mind assumptions are usually hidden and people will likely reveal them to their supervisor or leader only when the relationship supports honest, open communication without repercussion. In normal, everyday conversations, we are not typically used to another person challenging our thoughts and beliefs. It takes a high level of trust, a fair amount of skill, and a well-developed relationship to have the courage to challenge thoughts and beliefs and inspire a different outcome. A leader with a coaching style of leadership will develop these characteristics and successfully challenge and banish assumptions.

Challenging and banishing assumptions is achieved by first creating awareness that assumptions exist. Developing a trusting relationship first will enable leaders to learn the assumptions that are silent or hidden and lead the way to questions that challenge thinking. The key to banishing assumptions is action. Moving out of inaction or stagnation is accomplished by helping others notice that assumption might be false and new and different actions can lead to a new and different result.

> I discovered it wasn't a matter of physical strength, but of psychological strength. The conquest lay within my own mind to penetrate those barriers of self-imposed limitations and get through to that good stuff—the stuff called potential, 90 percent of which we rarely use.
>
> Sharon Wood, first North American woman to climb Mt. Everest, 1986

2

Have a Higher Purpose

My global mission is a world of peace where business is used to uplift the human spirit and alleviate poverty and suffering on our planet.

Dr. Mark Albion

My father passed away four months after he retired. He worked hard and long every day of his life. I remember him working three jobs at a time. I never once saw him asleep until his illness, in the hospital, when I was forty years old. He never lounged around in the morning. I don't remember him particularly enjoying his work. Work was something he felt he "had to" do, a responsibility.

He had a hard life with the youngest child having Prader-Willi Syndrome, a physical and mental impairment that wreaked havoc on our daily lives and limited our social life. I can't remember him having a hobby other than listening to jazz. He was waiting until he "had time," later. He hoped to move to Florida. What a dirty trick it seemed that he died right before he had a chance to truly enjoy his life. It never occurred to him to find meaningful work that made his heart sing, his soul happy and his life enjoyable every day.

Like so many people of his era, the Veterans Generation valued hard work, loyalty, and responsibility above all else. They didn't typically look for work they felt passionate about. Getting a good, secure job with a regular paycheck was the definition of success. It wasn't until later, until the Baby Boomer Generation grew up and went to work that they realized they wanted more. The Boomers wanted to make a difference; they wanted meaning and purpose.

When I began my work as a professional coach, I gathered a group of educators and engaged them in a reflective process to become their best leader. I introduced an activity that was to inspire them to think about their life goals. I asked them to get quiet and think about these questions:

- How do you want to be remembered for your life and work?
- What would you do if you had no limits?
- What would you do if you had unlimited support, resources, and courage?

I dimmed the lights and played some soft music. At the corner of my eye, I noticed one participant had tears flowing down her cheek. I wasn't prepared for her reaction. It seemed her mom had recently passed away. The questions hit home and hit her hard.

Death is a great teacher of life.

Over the last ten years as a professional coach, I realized how infrequently people ponder these big questions. I was surprised. I learned we are so busy thinking about here and now or the near future, this paycheck, and the next mortgage payment, that we spend little time giving ourselves permission to think beyond the immediate or near future. We choose a profession and get going with our lives and careers. Along the way, we become less interested or detached from our work, comfortably numb, maybe satisfied but not jazzed or passionately committed to much of anything, including our work.

The guiding values of the generations have shifted over the years, as well as how we look at life, at our chosen work, and creating meaningful, fulfilling lives. The Veterans were all about responsibility and security. The values that drove them left younger generations hungering for more—more meaning and greater sense of fulfillment. The Baby Boomer generation—the Me Generation—started to say *no* to the prevailing values of their parents. Women went to work, and lots of people went to encounter groups to find their lost selves. The personal growth business arose from people feeling desensitized about our unfulfilled lives. Then on to Generation X whose prevailing values system includes fun, thinking globally, and life-work balance. Nexters, or Generation Y, are an optimistic and confident bunch for whom fortune and fame are important. Over the years, it has become more important than ever to look deeply within to uncover what is most meaningful to us and bring it to fruition.

Why Purpose and Happiness Matter

Have you ever stayed in a job you loathed or changed jobs to seek more money or status, and then found it to be empty or a struggle? There's absolutely nothing wrong with taking such a job because you must put food on the table for your family. But that doesn't make the job especially meaningful to you. In my years of experience as a professional coach, I all too often worked with people who were let go from a job and were taken aback by it. When we drilled deeper to uncover the initial purpose for the job change, it was always a superficial reason: greater prestige, higher salary, to add to retirement income, for example.

When we follow what we are passionate about and what is meaningful to us, our positive energy drives us forward and leads to successful experiences, careers, and lives. The change you are seeking or the goal you are pursuing must be tied to a Higher Purpose. Here are some examples:

Goal	*Higher Purpose*
Be an effective leader	Ensure all staff members are achieving their potential
Run a marathon	Be a role model for my children
Start a nonprofit	Help families with critically ill children
Write a book about adoption	Help others feel free of rejection

Climbing the corporate ladder for increased status, salary, stature, or greater retirement income does not appear to lead to greater happiness or satisfaction. By 2020, the World Health Organization predicts depression will be the number two disease, second to heart disease. As the level of wealth in the United States has increased over several decades, the level of happiness has stayed constant. The chase for the buck may be causing greater stress and dissatisfaction than happiness (Dychtwald & Kadlec, 2009, p. 43).

In a study comparing happiness and income, the two countries with the highest happiness score, Denmark and Colombia, had widely varying average incomes. Guatemala scored the same as Canada, although average income was $4,700 versus $38,400. The United States was ranked 17th out of 94 countries. The impoverished population of Calcutta, living in crude shacks with little access to sanitary living conditions, is about even with Americans on the happiness scale. The things that do appear to reliably correlate with happiness are relationships and a sense of belonging to a community (Veenhoven, 2011).

Many of us have been programmed to believe that more money equates with more happiness. How then do we explain that among the poorest countries dwell the happiest people? When we are young and contemplating our career choices, we tend to think in practical terms—how much money we can earn to have the quality of life we wish—and off we go to pursue it. Somewhere along the line, we start to reexamine our lives and look differently at our definition of success; for many it happens when we reach middle age, between our fortieth to fiftieth birthdays. How we define success has a lot to do with expectations imposed by our families, friends, and the youthful innocence that may not know how to go about making choices that serve others and serve our soul. What does it feel like when you lack purpose? Do you feel empty, aimless, pointless, depressed, disengaged? Do you fill your empty soul with food, drugs, alcohol? What does your soul crave?

Numerous researchers have taken on the study of happiness and factors contributing to it. In *Authentic Happiness,* Martin Seligman (2002) condensed happiness components to three factors: (1) pleasure, things that feel good; (2) involvement, such as family and work; and (3) meaning, serving a higher good. According to a happiness survey developed by Professor Edward Diener in 2005 (Dychtwald & Kadlec, 2009, p. 57), the top three sources of happiness (78–80 percent) are the following:

- Relationship with family
- Friends and friendships
- Contributing to the lives of others

The bottom two sources of happiness (28–45 percent) are as follows:

- Job and career
- Amount of money earned

Jimmy Carter once said,

> Earlier in my life I thought the things that mattered were the things that you could see, like your car, your house, wealth, your property, your office. But as I've grown older, I've become convinced that the things that matter most are the things you can't see—the love you share with others, your inner purpose, your comfort with who you are. (quoted in Dychtwald & Kadlec, 2009, p. 50)

Expectations by others have had a tremendous influence on our career paths and choices we have made and in doing so have stifled many dreams. Choices based on extrinsic motivation factors such as prestige, earning a high salary, and status can leave us feeling empty. When we shift from making extrinsic choices to intrinsic ones, we achieve greater satisfaction with our lives and work. When we choose our life's work to align with our passion, unique talents, and drive to serve others, we achieve greater happiness. We are more authentic, more connected, more engaged, and more passionate about our chosen work.

What motivates you to do what you do and stay with it? Why did you choose your life's work? What factors are your primary motivators, those that keep you in your work or commitment toward your goal? The chart below identifies extrinsic versus intrinsic motivators.

Extrinsic Motivations	*Intrinsic Motivations*
Monetary compensation	Personal growth
Having power	Satisfaction of doing a good job
Having a title	Helping others develop
Public recognition	Finding meaning from efforts
Social status	Being true to one's beliefs
Winning over others	Making a difference in the world

Source: From *True North* (p. 107), by B. George, 2007, Hoboken, NY: Wiley. Copyright © Bill George. Reprinted with permission.

In *A New Earth*, Eckhart Tolle (2006) says we have both an inner and an outer purpose. Our outer purpose changes with circumstances, whereas our inner purpose remains always the same.

A coaching approach involves helping people create awareness of their Higher Purpose and aligning it with their everyday work. For educators, connecting meaning and purpose with what students are doing in the classroom will help motivate them.

As parents, educators, teachers, and guidance counselors incorporate a coaching approach, they will be equipped to guide youth to make inside-out choices versus outside in. By that I mean supporting them to not only explore their talents, gifts, and interests but to link them with a meaningful purpose. The same applies for leading staff. Engage people in conversations about identifying and connecting their meaningful purpose with their work. Having a meaningful Higher Purpose fosters greater depth and meaning for our personal lives, provides greater commitment to results at work, and increases satisfaction in all areas of our life.

Happier people with identified meaning and purpose are more engaged at work. To be fully engaged one must be physically energized, emotionally connected, mentally focused, and spiritually aligned.

What Is Your Mission?

> Everyone has trouble accepting the fact that he will disappear, unheard of and unnoticed in an indifferent universe.
>
> Milan Kundera

I bet many of you have seen or possibly helped create your organization's mission statement. You've likely seen it hanging on a wall or on your organization's annual report and never given it much thought beyond "That sounds nice." Think for a minute about the value of having a mission statement for your school district, your business, or your nonprofit organization. It should drive everything you do, help you select staff members who are aligned with your mission, and help you stay on track to meet your goals. It will help you say *yes* or *no* to new directions, strategies or actions. You already know this.

When we are seeking a change or are driven to reach a new or challenging goal, it is of significant importance to be able to identify the meaningful purpose of this big goal or change.

- What do I truly want to do? What must I do in my lifetime to feel I have made a difference?
- What will it do for others in the world (not just me)?
- How will it serve a greater good?

Have a Higher Purpose means keeping the big picture in mind, and identifying the good your goal or change will do for others. It is easy to forget why we are doing something and lose our purpose. People are more driven and likely to stay the course on the road to change when their efforts to change will ultimately make a difference or serve a common good.

> Fall in love with your life's work again or your energy will wane, your voice will falter and there will be nothing to prove but the fact that you are taking up valuable space.
>
> Anonymous

On an organizational level, leaders must keep the meaningful purpose at the forefront and communicate it constantly. More than this, you need to create a connection between an individual's Higher Purpose and the organization's purpose. Later in this chapter, we will focus on how to get started.

It's Not About the Soap

A great example of Have a Higher Purpose is a company in Boulder, Colorado, that began making soap using organic ingredients. The company, started in 2000 by a 23-year-old high school dropout, now generates a multimillion-dollar annual revenue and is a leader in the skin care market. One of the driving goals of Pangea Organics founder Joshua Onysko, was his vision to develop an education center, a nonprofit organization that would help corporations learn how to be more profitable through social responsibility and environmental sustainability. He started a skin care company to fund the Pangea Institute, an education center and small business incubator where classes and workshops on environmentally and socially responsible practices will be offered.

Pangea Organics is driven by Higher Purpose. Doing good for others has its rewards. Joshua's efforts and products, lauded by *Entrepreneur*, *O* (The Oprah Magazine) and *Time* magazines, have helped the company attract employees who feel equally inspired by the work.

Throughout Pangea's growth, Onysko never strayed from its mission: *Ecocentric Bodycare: Always Beneficial, Never Artificial*. Pangea hopes to reinvent the way we nurture our bodies and raise the bar for other companies. Return on investment has always been the bottom line driving most business plans. Not so at Pangea Organics. "We have the triple-bottom-line: people, profits and planet," says Onysko. When asked about the legacy he would like to leave, Joshua said, "I start each day by asking myself is my day being used to create a better world?" (Kahlili, 2009). I met Joshua at a farmer's market when I first moved to Boulder and have admired his success since 2003. His inspiration, youth, and passionate commitment have inspired me to donate a percentage of our company's revenue to nonprofit organizations, too.

Another inspiring example of Have a Higher Purpose is the work of the PassageWorks Institute, founded by educator and friend Rachael Kessler (2000). Her book *The Soul of Education* was a groundbreaking contribution to the field of social and emotional learning. For three decades, until the time of her death in 2010, Rachael partnered with colleagues around the country to develop an accessible language and framework that assists educators to address the inner lives of young people in schools. By "inner life," PassageWorks refers to that essential aspect of human nature that yearns for deep connection, grapples with questions about meaning, and seeks a sense of purpose, authenticity, and genuine self-expression. Throughout her time as executive director of PassageWorks, Rachael was also committed to broadening the leadership of the institute and creating a model that included the wisdom and experience of hundreds of educators around the country. A dedicated cohort of faculty and colleagues continues her legacy, collaborating with strategic partners around the country to offer a relationship-centered approach to teaching and learning.

A growing number of businesses are focusing on doing good for others and paying attention to social responsibility. Consumers seem to prefer doing business with companies that have a positive impact on their communities.

Years ago, I read *Diet for a New America* by John Robbins (1987), son of one of the founders of Baskin & Robbins Ice Cream. I learned about John's life and the choices he made to live a fulfilled life. He wrote about how he walked away from his family's fortune and a career in the ice cream business. He defied his father's goals for him, creating his vision and goals for his own life. One might wonder how anyone could walk away from easy street.

John saw his uncle Baskin develop hardening of the arteries resulting from his life and work choices. John chose to focus his life's work on healthy living choices. He founded EarthSave International (www.earthsave.org), an organization dedicated to healthy food choices, preservation of the environment, and a more compassionate world. John is also the board chair of YES! (www.yesworld.org), which educates, inspires, and empowers young leaders to take positive action for all life on Earth.

I attended a few lectures John gave and was impressed and inspired by the way he lives his life. He is a true example of one who chose to be guided by passionate commitment to a meaningful purpose over financial gain.

What Legacy Will You Leave Behind?

In *With Purpose*, Dychtwald and Kadlec (2009) believes we need another rung on Abraham Maslow's hierarchy of needs that better exemplifies life purpose—legacy. Legacy goes beyond self-actualization to

> a state of rich engagement where you take the best of who you are and the best of what you've cultivated over your life, and bring about meaningful involvement in activities and pursuits that lift up the sky for others as well as for yourself. (p. 57)

So what is your legacy? What do you want to survive of you?

On the night of the final dress rehearsal of the play *Rent*, Jonathan Larson, the 35-year-old composer and librettist, died of an aortic aneurysm. He worked on that play for seven years before it was produced. *Rent* went on to become the seventh longest-running Broadway show in history and won four Tony Awards and the Pulitzer Prize. Although his sudden death was a tragedy, he certainly left a legacy to be enjoyed for many more years.

> *I am what survives of me.*
>
> Erick Erikson

In *Living a Life That Matters*, Harold S. Kushner (2001) said,

> Most people are not afraid of dying; they are afraid of not having lived. What frightens them is the dread of insignificance, the notion that we will be born and live and one day die and none of it will matter. People understand that the story of their lives has a beginning, a middle, and an end. They desperately want to live long enough to get it right, to feel that they have done something worthwhile with their lives, however long. (p. 146)

Your legacy can be anything of importance: the songs or books you write, the work you do, the lives you touch, the goodness and smiles you spread one person at a time, the products you create, the warmth and love you give. We need to find and create meaning in the work we do, yet many of us have not been encouraged to think about doing work we are passionate about. Liking it used to be enough.

Tolerating it is far too common, leading to depression on the personal side and a disengaged workforce on the organizational side. There is a new way of working:

- Identify your higher purpose. (See Higher Purpose Tool 3.)
- Align your higher purpose with your work.
- Seek another line of work or organization if there is a disconnect.

Finding Meaning in Work and Life

Let us no longer be willing to separate work and life. They are interconnected. When staff members appear to lack commitment or seem burned out, leaders can be helpful by exploring what their purpose and passion are and discovering ways to create opportunities or alignment with them at work. We all want staff members who are emotionally connected and spiritually aligned with the work of the organization. Engaging in meaningful conversations will lead to more human organizations with people who care about one another.

If you have yet to think about your higher purpose, it is not too late. It never is. At different stages of our lives and careers, we can stop and ponder why we are doing what we do. Or we notice we are less enthusiastic than we used to be. Or something else is calling you.

> *Work is where the self meets the world.*
>
> David Whyte

What does the term *work* conjure up for you? Does the word inspire you? To me it used to imply drudgery, exertion, grind, sweat, and elbow grease. It's what I was told, taught and saw. What negative terms! To move us toward more satisfying lives and meaningful work, we need to reinterpret the term *work* itself to one that moves and inspires us. What if instead of viewing work as toiling away at something we are tolerating, we start to combine our talents and passionate interests and blend our professional work and personal lives in ways that enable us to contribute to others in a way of significant importance.

When the work you are doing has great meaning, you will experience greater positive energy that enables you to wake up each day happy and far less stressed. You are highly motivated, charged, ready to take on any challenges that arise. You feel unstoppable. Meaningful work equals motivated, dedicated, and engaged, joyful employees who are reliable, innovative, committed, and successful.

Leading Yourself and Others to Discover Their Higher Purpose

> *Until we make peace with our purpose, we will never discover true joy in our work or contentment in what we have.*
>
> *Richard J. Keider*

By now, I hope you see value to identifying a Higher Purpose. Let's take this concept a few steps further and explore how to start defining yours or revisiting it, and helping others do the same. While there are numerous ways to embark on processes to discover and uncover your purpose, this section will highlight two processes to help you get started:

- Finding joy
- Creating a personal mission statement

Finding Joy

What makes your heart sing? What gives you goose bumps? What moves your soul? What does joy feel like? Where and when do you fit joy into your life? Exploring the topic of joy was an eye-opener for me. I grew up content, but not joyful. I was raised with fear and limits. I struggled with this activity at first. We must find ways to bring joy and meaning to our lives and workplaces every day.

A few years ago, I was coaching Jenny, a new principal. She was overwhelmed by the job and although she loved it and was "happy," she began to notice she missed things she no longer had time to do. Specifically, she missed having time to paint. Jenny saw her "hobby" as something she had to do in her free time. After several coaching conversations, she began to recognize how much joy she found in creating, not just painting. We conjured up ways she could bring her creative side to work and carve out time after work to paint. Every day she identified new ways to be creative. No longer did she see spare time as her creative time. Every day became a creative process. She began adding some zest and graphics to her memos and brought in some inspiring photographs to line the walls of the school. Her happier state of being inspired others. She felt lighter. She emanated joy and it showed.

Often, we become so busy with everything we *have* to do, we forget to make time for what we *love* to do. Some people have yet to identify what they are passionate about. For years, every time I would ask my mom what she wanted for her birthday or where she and I might think about traveling to, she would say, "I have no wants." She had no dreams, nothing she wanted. The main thing and the only thing that mattered to her were the people in her life—doing things for them and spending time with them. All well and good except most of them had either moved away or were no longer living. Her thoughts were a result of being raised in an era when the purpose of work was solely to pay the bills and be a responsible person; people thought less about joy and happiness as a life priority. It is never too late to discover and bring joy to your days.

Look for the JoyFinder™ Tool. Do this when you are alone in a quiet place and have time to "go inner" and reflect on things that bring you joy. Go in nature if possible. In the left column, list twenty things you love. For example, you may write that you love to dance and hike, to be with your family, to watch a sunset, to travel, the smell of lavender, a tearjerker movie. You know when something brings you joy because you feel it in your heart and soul. Something resonates within you—goose bumps, happy tears, a stirring in your soul. In the right column, list how much time you will devote to each item in the next week. Feel free to use the JoyFinder™ Tool with staff, students, and with groups.

Happy people are happy employees. Their energy is up. Their attitudes are optimistic and more engaged at work and in life. Without joy, they are numb, unhappy, or even miserable. As a leader, don't you prefer staff members to be happy in their lives and happy at work?

> I'd rather be a failure at something I enjoy than a success at something I hate.
>
> George Burns

Your Life's Compass: Creating a Personal Mission Statement

Every credible organization has a mission statement that drives its purpose. It's why it exists. It defines who it serves. It keeps people on track and their goals and actions aligned to achieve it. It attracts the right leaders and employees who share the mission.

Individuals who wish to live a fulfilling life would be wise to create one for themselves. If you are already familiar with or experienced with the process of writing your organization's mission statement, take the same process and apply it to yourself first, then to others you lead.

While you may dabble in periodic thinking about the meaning of your life, most people don't have a visible personal mission statement. Why not create one? I highly recommend everyone devote some time and introspection to identify yours.

Writing a personal mission statement is a process to help discover your Higher Purpose. Your personal mission statement will drive your life. It will help you create or find work that is aligned with your purpose. It will serve as a guidepost and keep you focused on achieving it.

Your personal mission statement does many things:

- It acts as a compass to guide your life and life's work.
- It helps you define boundaries.
- It helps you make time for important priorities.
- It is focused on your future.
- It attracts people with similar dreams.
- It creates synergy and community.
- It defines who you are and what matters most to you.
- It defines what you are contributing to the world.

Although there are many ways to create a personal mission statement, you can begin by pondering these questions:

- Think about what you want to do: *What service do you want to offer others?*
- Think about whom you want to serve: *What segment of the population do you care about and want to help?*
- Think about why you want to do it: *What is my purpose?*

To continue, see Higher Purpose Tool 3. This is a personal, deep exploratory process. Resist the urge to get it done quickly. You can respond in sentences or paragraphs. It might take a few hours, days, or weeks to express your deepest desires. At the end of the process, synthesize your thoughts, dreams, and wishes into one or two powerful sentences. Martin Luther King's personal mission statement was "Equality for all . . . through peaceful means." It became his life work, and it is how he is remembered. A powerful mission statement includes your core values and future vision and addresses social responsibility.

I have heard some amazing life dreams and statements from our participants, such as, "I want to create a camp for empowering teenage girls." Here is an example of a statement by Heather, a physical education teacher, who was yearning to do something more:

Inspire teenagers to engage in physical challenges that will boost their confidence and teach healthy lifestyles.

Heather overcame some personal challenges and began running. Doing so empowered her to change her lifestyle and found many other positive changes ensued. She was enthused to share her experience with others. She started by gathering a group of teens and inspiring them to run a marathon.

By implementing Have a Higher Purpose, Heather was able identify why she wants to complete this goal. She wanted to make a difference in the lives of teenagers and be a role model for her own children. Heather had to get out of her comfort zone to connect with teenagers and encourage them to get involved. She had to deal with skeptical parents concerned their child might get hurt. She had to market the group and recruit participants. These were new and personal challenges for her, but because the higher purpose was meaningful to her, she persisted.

Your higher purpose should spark an emotional connection within you. Pay attention to your emotions when you think about the goal. What feelings will arise when you accomplish it? They are the energy source that will keep you connected and keep you moving forward, no matter what occurs prior to achieving it.

To become more effective at leading people to change, leaders must become skilled in helping people describe, define, and bring their higher purpose to life. You can begin by asking the questions found in the Have a Higher Purpose Tool 2. Help people identify how their passion and joy aligns with that of the organizations, or how it could align.

> To leave the world a bit better, whether by a healthy child, a garden path, or a redeemed social condition; to know that even one life has breathed easier because you lived. This is to have succeeded.
>
> Ralph Waldo Emerson

A Word About Courage

It is one thing to craft an inspiring higher purpose statement. It's an entirely other thing to bring it to life. It takes courage to live your dream and announce your meaningful purpose, instead of keeping it silent. Be gentle with yourself and others. Acknowledge the courage it takes to make the effort. Take consistent and persistent action steps, even if they are small. Be passionate; your energy will attract people who can be helpful in achieving the goal.

Many of us are taught to think small, to be nice, to be seen and not heard. It becomes easy to stop dreaming or never begin. That is the safe way. Living your purpose and having the courage to be who you are

> *Your playing small doesn't serve the world.*
>
> Marianne Williamson

and fully engaged in your Higher Purpose can feel risky at first. Growth is about breaking free from self-imposed limits and giving ourselves permission and the power to make our dreams come true. When they aligned with the greater good, they are pure and unselfish acts.

Dream as big as you can.

Tips for Success

- Take time to reflect on the meaning and purpose of your goal and life.
- Identify what you truly want to do and who the goal will serve.
- Do this process yourself before you lead others through it.
- Identify what you would do if there were no boundaries or perceived limits.
- Eradicate limiting thoughts before you begin.

Summary

I have proposed a heavy dose of inner work in this chapter. If "going inner" is new, begin with yourself. Expand the process to a few trusted colleagues, friends, or family members. Doing so will help you become more comfortable discussing Higher Purpose and personal mission statements with others.

It is becoming more mainstream to deeply consider the meaning of your life and to align your work, family, enjoyment, hobbies, and everything around it. It leads to great happiness. It also leads to individuals showing up at work happier, more engaged and more willing to work hard toward the common goals of the organization, especially when the individual's purpose is well aligned with the organization's purpose.

Don't wait for retirement. Embed joy and passionate purpose into your life every day and certainly into your work. Create a life where the line between work and joy is invisible.

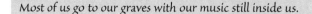

> *Most of us go to our graves with our music still inside us.*
>
> Oliver Wendell Holmes

3

Awareness of Limiting Thoughts

The only limit to our realization of tomorrow will be our doubts of today.

Franklin D. Roosevelt

If I had to pick one strategy essential for developing deep insight and know-how to foster change, it is this concept of how our inner thoughts limit what we do, or believe we are capable of achieving. The biggest key to change is within you. It is between your ears. It is your mind. It is those self-doubts, old stale beliefs, critical comments, and negative language we feed ourselves on a regular basis that impact what we do or don't do. It is not because of other people or other reasons that change does not occur. Our own poor habits of thought and negative self-talk are the culprit. Thoughts are not facts, but we often treat them as though they are true. We have the potential to transform ourselves, our circumstances, our perceptions, and our workplaces by creating awareness and intentionally changing our habitual, Limiting Thoughts.

I once had a client I will call Joe, who had made a recent job change to a higher leadership position. He was a confident successful leader and felt he had made the right decision at the right time in his career. Yet once he arrived in his new position, he felt a bit lost. He missed his former colleagues tremendously. He began to realize the importance of those relationships he cultivated for several years and began to question the decision he made to leave.

In the new position he felt less happy. He felt down. His energy was off. He was less effective and less fun to be around. He told himself, "I had it made there. I'll never find relationships like those again." Those very thoughts caused him to refrain from developing new relationships in his new environment. Once Joe began to notice how his thoughts held him back, he started to shift to a new plan of action, to reach out to his new central office colleagues and build a new community while maintaining his former relationships.

Limiting Thoughts are a major factor causing stagnation and resistance to change. Like assumptions, they are often silent. They are held in. A coaching approach to leading change must focus on how leaders can pay deep attention to what people are thinking, help them notice their effect, and shift them to uplifting thoughts.

What Are Limiting Thoughts?

You are today where your thoughts have brought you. You will be tomorrow where your thoughts take you.

James Allen

Limiting Thoughts are inner critical, negative voices and comments that swirl around in your head. Limiting Thoughts place self-imposed limits on what we believe we are capable of doing. Some call it monkey mind, limiting beliefs, inner critic, or automatic negative thoughts (ANTS). Limiting Thoughts are always negative. They drag us down just as assumptions do. They affect our spirit and sense of who we are as a person. I could write pages of Limiting Thoughts clients have shared with me. These comments are examples of those Limiting Thoughts:

- I can't sing.
- I am not a good writer.
- I am a terrible speaker.
- I stink at math.
- I don't have what it takes.
- I'll never get that promotion.
- I'm not a risk taker.
- I'm too short (tall, fat, or skinny).

- I failed before; I'll fail again.
- I'm not a detail person.
- I'm weak.
- I never finish anything I start.
- Good things happen for other people, never for me.
- I don't have enough time.
- I'll never pass the test.
- I don't have enough money.
- I don't have the support I need.
- I won't succeed.
- I can't change.
- I can't do it.
- I'm not creative.
- I can't dance (or sing, swim, etc.).

In *Embracing Your Inner Critic,* Hal and Sidra Stone (2003) describe the inner critic as "like the bit of mirror that makes us see a distorted picture. It is an inner voice that criticizes us and speaks about us in a disparaging way" (p. 4). Inner critical voices, or as I call them, Limiting Thoughts, stunt our growth and limit our options. Our inner critical voices have likely been with us since childhood, when we absorbed the fears, doubts, and limits we heard from the adults around us. We can go through the majority of our lives without even noticing these voices and the power they have over us. They rule us from within. They are like an inner judge who highlights anything and everything that is wrong with us. When we honor these voices and act as if the voices are correct, we limit ourselves and our ability to grow, change, evolve, stretch, take risks. We stay stuck.

In *Magnificent Mind at Any Age,* Dr. David Amen (2008) identifies nine types of Limiting Thoughts he calls ANTS (automatic negative thoughts) (p. 172):

- Always thinking; overgeneralizing
- Focusing on the negative
- Fortune telling; predicting a negative future
- Mind reading; arbitrarily believing you know what someone else thinks
- Thinking with your feelings; believing negative feelings without questioning them
- Guilt beatings; using words like *should, must, ought, have to*
- Labeling; attaching a negative label to yourself or others
- Personalization; allowing innocuous events to take on personal meaning
- Blame; blaming others for problems in your life

Identify a Limiting Thought you have or heard from someone else.

_____

_____

_____

How has it stopped you or impeded progress toward the goal?

_____

_____

_____

Our inner thoughts are key to whether we will move toward a desired change or not. If we consistently tell ourselves "I can't do that" there is little likelihood we will try. No effort equals no change. When leaders adopt a coaching style of leadership, they learn to work with Limiting Thoughts, helping others become aware of them and shift thoughts from "I can't" to "I can," from "I won't" to "I will." Positive thoughts have been very strongly linked to achieving goals. People with a positive attitude strive and stay committed to achieving their goals and often surpassing them.

Change is an individual process for each person. Leaders need to consider how each person thinks about the change or goal and work with each one to create the awareness and make the shifts necessary to get from where that person is to where he or she wishes to go. No more groupthink. Just as with assumptions, leaders need to develop trusting relationships in which staff members feel free to share their inner thoughts.

> Ninety-five percent of beliefs we have stored in our mind are nothing but lies, and we suffer because we believe in these lies.
>
> Don Miguel Ruiz

The good news is we can change those thoughts! Contrary to common belief, unproductive, negative thoughts don't have to reside in your mind forever. You don't own them although you might be (overly) attached to them. They don't have to define you. You don't have to keep them, especially the ones that cause you to stifle yourself, limit your potential, and create stagnation. Most of the time we don't challenge or question them.

> *Nurture great thoughts. You will never go higher than your thoughts.*
>
> Benjamin Disraeli

Most people don't realize they can change them. You can easily change your thoughts, even those you have held on to for aeons.

Managing Limiting Thoughts and Beliefs

Some of us have held on to these stale thoughts for our lifetime. Without thinking about them, we continue to tell ourselves these negative, draining thoughts, which we come to believe as true. Stop for a moment and think about the impact of your Limiting Thoughts. In organizations, it is common to keep those thoughts to oneself and never air them.

Ashley, a principal in a school with a long history of a negative culture, was concerned about Terry, a teacher and union president. Their relationship was distant and had been for a long time. Ashley wanted it to improve and wanted Terry to be a more positive influence in the building. Trouble was Ashley had such a long-held Limiting Thought that Terry will never change and she did nothing to improve it. She could not see possibilities. She avoided Terry instead of considering other strategies. With a coaching approach, Ashley began to focus on what she wanted to accomplish and learned to squash her own negative thoughts that were in the way of taking positive action steps.

Thoughts become beliefs. Without a method for turning around the negative thoughts that prevail, they become habitual thoughts. There is very likely to be no truth to these beliefs. They are just old thoughts that hold us back.

If you are seeking a change for yourself, your organization, or your team, you must intervene and learn how to reverse these negative thoughts. In challenging organizations such as school systems (as well as any organization), this concept of Limiting Thoughts can make such a radical difference in the lives of students, teachers, and school leaders. When staff members can learn to work with those damaging thoughts, and help people switch those thoughts to unlimited thinking, students, teachers, and leaders will discover this strategy has the potential to make the changes they have been seeking—the ability to overcome resistance to change and reach even greater levels of thinking. It can and will be a turnaround concept that leads to possibility thinking instead.

One small word can create a huge and profound shift. To manage Limiting Thoughts, turn them around from negative to positive, from *no* to *yes*. This is a significant step in making inside-out authentic change. Begin to notice your Limiting Thoughts. How often do you think a particular thought? In what ways does it stop you?

> The difference between can and cannot are only three letters. Three letters that determine your life's direction.
>
> Remez Sasson, Author

Lilly once told me, "I'm not very good at politics." She hired me to pursue getting her first job as a superintendent. She also told me she was an introvert who was encouraged to pursue the job because of her success as an assistant superintendent for instruction. She loved professional development, working with teachers, and creating success for students.

Moving to the next level required her to consider her strengths and confront areas in which she lacked confidence. She was well aware of aspects of her personality that would potentially hold her back. She knew being an introvert would challenge her every day on the new job, and she became increasingly anxious. She had a love of curriculum and developing programs and strategies that would help students succeed. She deeply disliked the idea of "kissing up" to people to win them over. She viewed that as insincere. For Lilly to pursue the superintendency and be successful in it, she had to look at how her Limiting Thoughts were holding her back. She began to reframe how she viewed aspects of the position, from thoughts that caused anxiety to thoughts that inspired and energized her.

In another case, Margaret, a client of one of our coaches-in-training slowly began to unlock her self-imposed limits and started reading her poetry in public. For years, she knew she had talent and love for writing. She imposed limits on herself for fear success would threaten her marriage. She began to notice her level of unhappiness by containing her natural talent. After a few weeks of coaching, Margaret blossomed and began to actively pursue public poetry readings with joy.

When we become aligned with our gifts and true purpose, we give ourselves permission to be all we can be. We break free. We release the limits of our past thinking.

The Power of Choice

One of the mistakes we make is to accept our own Limiting Thoughts without question. If individuals have beliefs about themselves that they are distractible, they tend to carry on with that behavior. We often think our behavior is permanent: "That's just the way I am." We refrain from taking the time and energy needed to change behavior that is counterproductive to the changes we want.

One of the most powerful concepts in a coaching approach is that we always have a choice. We can choose our thoughts, our beliefs, and our actions. We can instantly change those thoughts, beliefs, and actions at any time. We can break free of thoughts that have held us back and adopt fresh ways of thinking that support us in moving forward. This is the heart of coaching, and the heart of making lasting change, at last!

How to Change Limiting Thoughts to Expanding Thoughts

Leaders need to become aware of and skilled in shifting Limiting Thoughts to unlimited thoughts. The quality of our thinking influences and impacts everything we do— our relationships, career success, how we look at our lives overall. An abundance of negative thinking and self-Limiting Thoughts affects our hormone system, our brain, and our

> *The difficulty lies not so much in developing new ideas as in escaping from old ones.*
>
> John Maynard Keynes,
> British economist

physical body. Our thoughts, like everything else, are an energy source. How do you feel, physically, when you consistently feed yourself negative, critical thoughts?

To shift Limiting Thoughts to unlimited, expanding thoughts follow these four steps:

1. Create an awareness of Limiting Thoughts.

2. Notice their frequency and impact.

3. Create a turnaround statement.

4. Repeat the turnaround statement often.

Step 1: Creating Awareness of Limiting Thoughts

Consistent negative thoughts on a frequent basis are a sure formula for failure. We can't change what we can't see, or what we are unaware of. A coaching approach means conscious creation of our future. We become acutely aware of what we are thinking, in the moment, and consider if our habit of thinking is helping or hurting our goal or change we want. Leaders with a coaching approach will listen deeply to what one is saying. They listen for Limiting Thoughts that get in the way of the goal.

Bob, a principal, is meeting with a teacher whom he wants to encourage to be more effective dealing with irate parents. The teacher, Irene, resists making the calls, causing the parent to call the principal instead. Irene is a new teacher, even-tempered with a lifelong history of avoiding uncomfortable conversations. Bob has had many phone calls from parents and wants Irene to step up to the plate and make the calls herself. It is time for Irene to face the music and make a change. Irene has made a few feeble attempts, such as calling when she knows the parent isn't home. She always cowered from anger. The principal hears Irene say things like, "I'm not good at confronting people when they are angry." "I freeze when someone is yelling at me." Irene and Bob have a good relationship and Irene feels comfortable being honest with him.

In order for Bob to help Irene and coach her to a better resolution, he first asked her to notice her Limiting Thoughts. Irene needs to become aware of what she thinks, and how often these comments surface and cause her to stagnate. Frequency impacts this formula for failure. When Irene thinks of calling the parent, she begins to notice certain thoughts:

- I'll make a fool of myself.
- I'll sound like a wimp.
- I feel defensive.
- I can't hide my lack of experience.

Notice how all of these thoughts are negative and disempowering. They would hardly bolster one's confidence. Notice how the problem lies within Irene's inner thoughts. The solution to the problem is not the parent's mood or anger. It is Irene and her ability and willingness to change her Limiting Thoughts to those that will support her to develop her confidence muscles and deal more effectively with irate parents. Irene shifted her Limiting Thoughts from those above to these:

- I am a successful communicator.
- I sound confident.
- The parent will respect me.
- I am becoming more comfortable with every call.

Irene's new thoughts are empowering, uplifting, and positive. With repetition, over time they will become her default thoughts and she will no longer hide from calling parents.

A coaching approach means helping people notice when and how their thoughts are limiting them and creating the obstacle to change. A leader with a coaching approach is one who listens for what is in the way of success, and communicates that, along with the ability to change what is currently not working, to find an approach that will support the change. You are not telling people what they should do. You are helping them notice what they are doing that is blocking success. You are helping them create awareness, and recognize that frequency adds to the problem.

Creating awareness is the first step. To help create awareness of their Limiting Thoughts, individuals can . . .

- Listen deeply for Limiting Thoughts.
- Tell someone when they hear a Limiting Thought. For example, "I heard you say you could never create close relationships with your new colleagues."

A coaching approach to change involves looking deeply at thoughts and their frequency and developing a plan to reformat them. You can help staff members discover for themselves the new thoughts, beliefs, and perceptions that strengthen their ability to take action and achieve what is important to them.

Step 2: Notice the Frequency

Challenge people to become aware of their limiting beliefs. Ask them to make a mental note every time they hear their critical inner voice feeding them a negative message. I find it helpful to write them down and begin to notice how often they arise. Write all of them down in a list. Each time we hear a Limiting Thought repeated, keep track of how often it occurs by using a tick mark. Doing this also reinforces Step 1 by creating greater awareness of their frequency.

Step 3: Create a Turnaround Statement

The way to change Limiting Thoughts to unlimited, expanding thoughts is to create a *turnaround statement*. The turnaround statement is the new response, the new voice that people will say to themselves every time the (old) Limiting Thought comes to mind. Writing turnaround statements can take time and practice. (See Examining Limiting Thoughts Tool in the Tools section of this book.)

The new turnaround statement is positive, energizing, and creates a picture of the preferred state, as if it already exists. Turnaround statements reflect the opposite thinking. It doesn't matter if that thinking doesn't exist yet. With repetition, it will become the automatic response.

Here are some examples:

Limiting Thought: I have nothing really important to say.

Turnaround statement: I have a lot to contribute to this project.

Limiting Thought: I am a terrible writer.

Turnaround statement: I am acquiring the skills to improve my writing.

These are sample questions for creating Awareness of Limiting Thoughts:

- How does that belief hold you back?
- What might be the benefit of letting go of that belief?
- How often do you tell yourself that?

Step 4: Repeat Often

Once a satisfactory turnaround statement is created, memorize it or have it available so it can be repeated often and every time the old statement tries to sneak in. It may feel forced at first. Just go with it. You are reprogramming your brain to create unlimited expanding thoughts!

A Formula for Freedom

Consider for a moment what it would be like and feel like to be completely free of Limiting Thoughts. When we suddenly cease from stagnating and draining our energy through these self-Limiting Thoughts, we become free. We are free of self-imposed boundaries and can now fulfill our unlimited potential with an abundance of new, positive energy flowing from our thoughts!

Make a habit of this process, and you have unlocked a very important key to change.

Direct Your Brain to Change

All of the strategies in this book are those used by professional coaches. Coaching strategies are aligned with research and discoveries about how our brain functions. We can be a CHANGEMASTER by understanding and applying them. In past years, it was thought that the brain was fixed, that we

> *Our thoughts have a real, measurable, negative biological impact on brain function.*
>
> David Amen, MD

were stuck with what we were born with. Research has shown this to be wrong. Science writer Sharon Begley's (2007) book *Train Your Mind, Change Your Brain* offers ground-breaking documentation to support the idea that we can change our brains by changing our thoughts. These breakthroughs in our understanding show it is possible to "reset our happiness meter, regain the use of limbs disabled by stroke, train the mind to break cycles of depression and OCD, and reverse age-related changes in the brain," according to the publisher.

Thoughts, feelings, and actions determine the health of our brain. Our brain never loses its power to transform itself based on what it experiences. We have also learned our brain can transform over very short intervals. Your brain is different today than it was yesterday. This difference results from yesterday's experiences, as well as the thoughts and feelings you've had over the past day. Your brain is a lifetime work in progress.

We have learned from scientific research that we can all become a prodigy with repeated practice. We have no limits other than those we impose on ourselves. Findings indicate that following certain brain-based guidelines, anyone can achieve expert performance in sports, academics, music or art. Peak performers are made, not born! People with extraordinary abilities have learned to use their brains differently than the average person.

We are all filled with infinite potential. This has profound implications on how we attempt change personally, professionally, and organizationally. It has profound implications for educators who must believe in infinite potential for every student, for leaders who must believe in the possibility of our challenging goals, for every teacher to believe every student can learn.

Anders Ericsson, a psychologist from Florida State University, who studied geniuses, prodigies, and other superior performers in sports, arts, and entertainment, is convinced that there are no special inherited qualities that distinguish persons with expert abilities. Ericsson, Prietula, and Cokely say,

> The development of genuine expertise requires struggle, sacrifice, and honest, often painful self-assessment. There are no shortcuts. It will take you at least a decade to achieve expertise, and you will need to invest that time wisely, by engaging in "deliberate" practice—practice that focuses on tasks beyond your current level of competence and comfort. You will need a well-informed coach not only to guide you through deliberate practice but also to help you learn how to coach yourself.

No longer do we have to accept such comments as, "I don't have what it takes" or "I have no will power." You can choose and change thoughts just as you chose what shirt to wear today. When you choose a brand new thought, you are creating new circuits in our brain. When repeated over time, that thought becomes our new go-to thought. Change your thoughts and you change brain function.

When thoughts are predominantly negative, you feel bad. Positive helpful thoughts cause you to feel good. No wonder chronically negative thoughts are so damaging. I heard it once said that 80 percent of our thoughts per day are negative ones. We have to consciously work at shifting them to positive thoughts, until those positive thoughts prevail.

Thoughts are very powerful. Our brain and body react to each and every one. Every thought causes the release of chemicals and an electrical transmission across your brain, creating awareness of your thought. When you feel sad, annoyed, hopeless, or angry, you release negative chemicals and you feel bad. Notice how your body feels when you are in a negative thought. Your muscles tighten, blood pressure rises, breathing rate increases, and your heart beats faster.

When you have positive, happy, uplifting, kind thoughts, the chemicals released by your brain make you feel good. Notice how you feel when you think them. Your body reacts by relaxing the muscles; breathing is slower and deeper and blood pressure goes down and slows your heart rate.

Every cell is affected by every thought. Unless you consciously focus on your thoughts most of them are automatic. And since the majority of our thoughts are negative, we must pay specific attention to them so we can observe them and reprogram them to positive ones. We must learn to combat the negative thoughts and replace them with positive ones.

It is estimated that 95 percent of mental behavior is subconscious and automatic (Iyengar, 2010, p. 167). We must be mindful and aware of how our thoughts, feelings, and actions create the reality we live. If we want a different reality we must start by addressing our inner thoughts, being aware of our subconscious mind, and exercising control. Suppose you are walking to a meeting at a certain pace. You look at your watch and notice you'll be late if you continue to walk at this pace. You tell yourself to pick up the pace. You tell your brain to speed it up, and it does. In just the same way, you can tell your brain anything, and it will respond accordingly. "Ultimately, our walking speed can be under our conscious control, just as our body language, facial expressions and style of speech can, but unless we make an effort to continually exercise control, we will defer to the dictates of the automatic system" (Iyengar, 2010, p. 167).

> *You are never given a dream without also being given the power to make it true. You may have to work for it, however.*
>
> *Richard Bach, Author*

Tips for Success

- Be conscious of every word you hear and speak.
- Recognize that people have the ability to change their thoughts.
- Replace negative words and statements with uplifting ones.
- Create turnaround statements that support the goal.
- Rehearse turnaround statements often.

Summary

Leaders of change must become skilled in leading people to successful change by learning to working with Limiting Thoughts. When our thoughts change, we are free to change our actions. When we repeat our actions, over time, we have created new habits. We create new habits when we tell our brain we are doing something new; we change the patterns in our brain. They become embedded as new habits when they are repeated.

When we hold on to Limiting Thoughts, they take over. They drive what we do or don't do. Leaders and individuals seeking change must be attentive and conscious of their thoughts and those of others. Thoughts can be changed by choosing different ones. New thoughts become the new constant thought with repeated practice of turnaround statements created to banish negative thoughts. Leaders must become skilled in helping people shift from negative to positive thoughts, from stagnating to empowering ones.

4

Nix the Negatives
and Naysayers

Perception is real even when it is not reality.

Edward de Bono,
Psychologist and Author

Would you agree the hardest aspect of a leader's job is dealing with negative people and resistance from individuals or groups of them? People skills are more important to your success as a leader than your depth of knowledge, how many degrees you have, and your years of experience. Success as a leader depends upon your successful intervention with negativity.

I have witnessed many leaders who avoid negativity and negative situations rather than confront them. They run for the hills or hide out in their office. I vividly remember a tragic story that happened in the organization I worked for almost twenty years. Rose was our office manager. She was bright, extremely capable, and a classic underachiever with numerous physical ailments, including chronic back pain, severe allergies, weight, and emotional issues. Her home life was unhappy; she struggled with her marriage and making ends meet.

Rose liked coming to work. It was an escape and haven for connection and self-worth. When she was promoted to office manager, other clerical staff members began to exclude her from lunch and coffee breaks. They were openly hostile toward her, causing Rose began to feel ostracized. Her immediate supervisor was aware of the situation, but was not the supervisor for the other office workers. The director of our division was aware of the situation, but took no action to remedy it. He was not one to confront.

One day I arrived at work and noticed many people whispering in the halls. There was an odd feeling in the air. The day before, Rose overheard some cruel remarks about her made by her former peers. She took them to heart, proceeded to her desk, and emailed everyone a suicide note. She went home for lunch and died from an intentional overdose of drugs.

This is an extreme example. I cannot help but wonder that if the leadership intervened and dealt with the negativity in the office, Rose would not have felt so desperately alone. Negativity must be dealt with. We cannot shy away from it. We must become more comfortable having conversations that get to the heart of issues.

Negativity can squash your goals. It can spread to other people and create waves of opposition. Negativity is a powerful and damaging force.

Be Wary of Your Words

You know how easily we can either respond to someone's warm welcome or be repelled by a chilling word. Our words either draw people to us or push us away. Inner thoughts generate our outer words.

One encouraging word to someone who is in a negative frame of mind might be just the thing needed to help that person deal with a problem or shift in attitude. On the other hand, a negative word to someone already struggling can keep that person down. Pay attention to every spoken word and the meaning it conveys. Are your words supporting and uplifting or negative and draining? Begin to think about what you do when you hear other people's negative words. How do you respond?

People seem to seek others who think like they do. Think about statements such as "Like attracts like" and "Misery loves company." People voice their complaints, find a rationale for unhappiness, and seek or attract other people who agree with them. They might feel empowered or right if so-and-so shares his or her thoughts and ideas, too. We sometimes connect with others through our similar thoughts.

Bands of individuals bond together with negative thoughts can squelch your goals. Resistance occurs, expands, and multiplies by masses of people who jump on the negativity bandwagon and altogether feel they are right. Along comes someone telling them to change. It is surely a leadership challenge to move the thoughts, attitudes, and opinions of the masses.

Consciously or unconsciously, we choose which words spoken by others we will follow or align with. We can choose to agree or disagree. If our opinions are the same, we will agree and align ourselves with that person. But when we make an effort to change our language, our perception of a situation will gradually change, usually for the better. You might be shocked to stop and listen to yourself (or others) speak. The amount of negative language you hear would probably alarm you. Start by listening to yourself, to your thoughts, to your conversations with others, and learn to identify negative language.

Become aware of the negative language you tell yourself, or that your staff, students, or friends say. What words do you feed yourself? What words or doubts are others feeding you? A diet of doubt will not get you to your goal. Back off from people who negate your ideas. Surround yourself with people who are enthused and will support you. Don't let negative energy drain your positive energy. Negative language is useful data. It is a gift that gives you direct, specific insight into what someone thinks. Words are powerful. They can create an outcome or destroy one.

Last year I was planning a trip to Thailand. I knew two people who'd been there before. One told me that Bangkok was the dirtiest, filthiest city she'd ever seen. She couldn't wait to leave. Another found it fascinating. I went anyway. I found Bangkok to be busy, congested, crowded, noisy, dark, and at the same time captivating, intriguing, bustling with life and culture, filled with hardworking people who seemed to be enjoying life. I loved Bangkok.

Think of the words we use as an energy source. They can be charged with positive energy or with draining energy. Monitor your words and exchange words that zap energy with words that inspire. This may take some practice. See the A to Z Uplifting Words Tool for a list of positive, uplifting words.

How We Connect

In business or our personal lives, we encounter negative people regularly. If we are like them, we will hang out with them. If we are seeking a change or leading it, we must become adept at sniffing out negativity and shifting it to the positive.

We connect through our likes and dislikes, our preferred activities, values, beliefs, and shared experiences. We communicate our ideas, solutions, goals, and expectations through our words, body language, and facial expressions. Language is core, basic to our existence. It is the tool we use to express ourselves and form relationships with others.

Humans have a natural instinct to connect with one another. The need and desire for connection is so great that many people might prefer to compromise their thoughts and individuality to remain connected with others, even when it is unproductive to do so.

Or there might be a case of "groupthink" occurring behind the scenes. *Groupthink*, a term coined by social psychologist Irving Janis in 1972, occurs when a group makes faulty decisions because of group pressures. People affected by groupthink ignore alternatives. They may try to minimize conflict and reach consensus without critically testing, analyzing, and evaluating ideas (Janis, 1982). Individual creativity, uniqueness, and independent thinking can get lost in the pursuit of group cohesiveness. During groupthink, members of the group avoid promoting viewpoints outside the comfort zone of consensus thinking. They may do this for a variety of reasons: to avoid being seen as foolish, to avoid embarrassment, or to avoid angering other members of the group.

> *Inside of a ring or out, ain't nothing wrong with going down. It's staying down that's wrong.*
>
> Muhammad Ali

Confronting Negatives and Naysayers

It is said that the mind processes fifty thousand to eighty thousand messages a day, including those we read, hear, and think about and that 80 to 90 percent of them are negative ones! No wonder we think change is hard. No wonder it seems we are battling the odds or fighting our way through the sea of negativity. We are!

In a group setting, negativity can zap the energy in no time flat. It reduces participation, erodes teamwork, and diminishes the value of the topic of conversation. If you are the speaker, leader, or facilitator, it is better to be prepared, to beef up your leadership muscles and to develop skills to shift negative energy to positive energy.

If you let yourself and others be dragged down by doubts, fears, and limiting thoughts, you will never get to your goal. You will need to listen to your own voice, your own deep commitment to the goal. To achieve your change or goal, you need to become acutely aware of your own spoken words and those of others. Notice negative ones and how frequent they are present.

It takes a great deal of personal strength and determination to confront resistant staff. You must stand tall. A coaching approach style of leadership helps leaders realize it is possible to break through negative thinking and make progress with resistant staff members. Remember the guiding principle that thoughts can be changed.

Be a Better Listener

There seems to be a growing crisis for human beings to be heard, truly and sincerely listened to. Most people feel unheard and crave to be engaged in meaningful relationships. Feeling heard helps us feel understood and validated by others. We feel more connected and less isolated when we feel safe to reveal our thoughts without judgment.

Listening is the foundation of all relationships and can be an essential factor between a relationship being meaningful or not. I believe a great deal of naysaying is the craving to be heard. We can remedy that by becoming better listeners.

Listening well is another crucial skill for leaders to master. Staff members are overwhelmed with external pressures and busy personal and professional lives. Becoming a better listener improves the level of trust between you and others.

List those people you would identify as good listeners.

_____

_____

_____

What did they do to make you feel that way?

_____

_____

_____

It is obvious that when you engage in a conversation with someone who truly listens, it creates a unique connection, relationship, and bond with that person. I often ask clients and groups to consider the above questions. All too often, I have witnessed sadness and tears as people recognize the lack of connection and relationship with someone who listens to them.

It is said that adults spend about 70 percent of their waking time communicating. This is how that breaks down:

- 14 percent is spent in writing
- 16 percent is spent in speaking
- 17 percent is spent in reading
- 53 percent is spent in listening

With more than half our time spent in listening, it gets the least amount of instruction. No wonder people feel detached, disengaged, and "unheard!" Count your blessings if you have been fortunate enough to have had a deep listening partner in your life: a friend, spouse, boss, or colleague. Chances are, if you have, you noticed it was likely a special relationship. As a leader with a coaching approach, a significant function of your role is to engage in deep, attentive, focused, and active listening. Doing so will diminish the effect of negative people and decrease resistance to change.

Becoming a great listener isn't automatic. Hearing is automatic; listening is an intentional process. Most conversations are shallow levels of speaking and listening. To master successful change, you must be willing and skilled to go to deeper levels of listening. Taking time to do so will result in more honest and trusting relationships that will enable leaders to turn naysayers into positives.

There are many possible reasons people don't listen well:

- They are disinterested in the issue or person.
- They are bored.
- They are too busy.
- They are distracted.
- They don't value the speaker's thoughts, ideas, or contributions.
- They are thinking of what to say next.
- They think the message is too complex.

To listen is to pay attention, to care, to take the time to suspend our own thoughts, to-do lists, and concerns, to acknowledge and validate what another is feeling. Speaking and listening are like a dance where partners take turns; one speaks, one listens. But all too often, listeners are not really listening. They are busy thinking of what to say, or connecting to a similar experience, instead of shifting attention to the speaker and focusing on what that person thinks and feels.

> The need to be heard, which is something we ordinarily take for granted, turns out to be one of the most powerful motives in human nature. Being listened to is the medium through which we discover ourselves as understandable and acceptable. The good listener appreciates us as we are, accepting the feelings and ideas we express as they are. In the process we feel understood, acknowledged and accepted. (Nichols, 2009, p. 18)

There is power in the words we speak. An encouraging word to someone who is down can be just the sort of thing to help him make it through a problem. By contrast, a negative word to someone who is struggling to reach higher ground can be just the sort of thing to keep him in a pit of despair. Listen deeply to every word, for words are the indicators of attitudes, beliefs, and the source of resistance.

It would serve you well to increase your attentive listening to others. You may witness the ripple effect of negative people in the workplace diminish. Be willing to give people the gift of your attention and allow them time and space to be heard. You do not have to fix them or their problem as they see it. They simply may want an ear, and once they feel heard, they can be more open to consider options.

When people feel unheard, they are likely to do or experience some of the following:

- Complain
- Detach
- Disengage
- Feel lonely
- Feel disconnected
- Align with others who feel as they do

Suppose you have a high percentage of people on your staff that you think are resistant to change. Instead of viewing them as unchangeable, you can get to the root cause of their resistance by approaching them one person at a time. Doing this will give you the change to learn why they are resisting change.

Listening deeply is a caring act. When you are listening deeply, you can feel many different things:

> Not being listened to is hard on the heart, and so to varying degrees we cover our need for understanding and mechanisms of defense.
>
> Michael P. Nichols, Author

- Connected
- Engaged
- Cared about
- Valued

Hearing + Attention + Heart = Listening Deeply

I encourage you to pay attention to the level of listening that you engage in on a regular basis. Are you in too much of a hurry to deeply listen? Do you feel too tied to your opinion? Your busy-ness is likely an aspect of the problem keeping you from connecting with others on a deeper level. Listening deeply will most certainly boost your relationships with people and erode the defensive walls some hold on to. Listening deeply is achieved by hearing what one is saying with focused, undistracted attention, and listening with your heart, listening beyond spoken words.

Practical Ways to Nix the Negatives

Below are some specific responses leaders can use when they encounter negative language:

- *I can't*—This type of thinking will stop people before they start. Ask if it is true that they really cannot, or is it that they never tried.
- *I failed before*—This type of thinking will inhibit future attempts and progress will not be made. Help people learn to see a past negative experience as something that helped them grow and encourage them to keep trying until they are successful. There is no such thing as failure, only failed attempts.
- *I never*—Someone who thinks this way is closed to seeing possibilities. Challenge this thinking with such questions as these: Where did this type of thinking come from? What makes you believe this? What if that were not so? Equip yourself with stories of achievement and accomplishment.

- *I'll try*—This is a sure sign the person will likely *not* try. When we tell ourselves "I'll try" it leaves an escape clause. Request words that imply commitment. People are either going to do something or not.

Here are some additional strategies to consider:

- Choose words with care. Consciously upgrade your language to include words that are positive and empowering (see A to Z Uplifting Words Tool).
- Empathize. Negative people will benefit from an empathetic ear rather than giving them suggestions or solutions. It can be helpful to offer empathy prior to asking questions that challenge their thinking.
- Stick to positive topics. Refrain from letting yourself get dragged into negative discussions.
- Let negative comments roll off your back. Practice nonjudgment and lower your own defenses.
- Learn to reframe. Help negative people see the change or challenge from a new perspective. Ask questions that are open-ended and cause them to explore their thoughts.

Reframing: A Powerful Skill

Have you ever painted a room a different color and noticed it evoked a whole different feeling? Did you ever change the color of the mat surrounding a picture and notice how it looks so different? The used car industry has helped sell old cars by cleverly calling them previously owned instead of used.

Reframing is a strategy for spinning something one believes is negative into something positive. It means shifting perception. The concept of reframing is essential for creating transformational change.

While we do want to respect, acknowledge, and honor other people for their views and perceptions, we also need to become acutely aware of the damaging perceptions that are in the way of success.

> *Progress is impossible without change and those who cannot change their minds cannot change anything.*
>
> George Bernard Shaw

Reframing how we view situations is a key skill for leaders or individuals who want to achieve a change. We have to gain a new viewpoint. From an old viewpoint, we can't change. The person mentioned earlier will not appreciate Bangkok unless she can let go of that dirty, negative lens through which she views the city. Reframing is a way that we can alter our perceptions and see negative events as a learning experience instead.

When People Won't Budge

On the other hand, after you tried all the tricks in the book and are unable to make headway with certain individuals, your next best step is to surround yourself with positive people. Back off and back away. Do not let yourself be influenced by negative energy and negative words. While it may sound easy, in reality it can be quite difficult to distance yourself from people who have been in your circle, your work team, or your world. It may hurt. It may cause confusion as you make a move to align yourself with people who are open to change.

According to well-known research on diffusion of innovation by Everett M. Rogers (2003), a scholar of communication and social change, typically, 16 percent of a group will remain negative and refuse to budge from their opinion. These laggards prefer to keep the status quo. They are closed to new ideas, new strategies, or new goals. When you are certain you have tried all the strategies to support them to change, be willing to let go of the possibility they might change. Focus your energy on those who will budge. As the song by All American Rejects says, "Move along, move along." Another group, the late majority, makes up about 34 percent of a group and is skeptical of a change and relies on trusted advisors or leaders. These two groups are about 50 percent of a staff. Half of your staff members are at some level of resistance. Some can be inspired to change; some cannot (p. 281).

Cultivating Optimism

I love to share stories of people who have overcome the odds, have done something that appears super human, or stretches our perceived limits. Leaders need to combat negative thinking among staff members and cultivate optimism and positive thinking, by having some success stores in their bag of tricks. Here's a favorite of mine.

How would you react if I said, "I am going to run five marathons back-to-back in fifty days?" What would you say? It's likely you'll tell me I'm nuts. You might think, "That is completely impossible. No one can do that."

A few years ago, having never been a runner before, I decided to start. I joined a running club and ran a few local 10k races. I was suddenly in awe of anyone who ran more than that. One night I attended a talk in a local running store. The speaker was Dean Karnazes. I had not heard of him before. I just wanted to learn more about running. I was so proud of myself then for running for forty-five straight minutes. What I heard astounded me.

I heard Dean talk about running "ultra-marathons." Little did I know then, he had just published a book, *Ultra Marathon Man.* He talked about running five marathons in a row, nonstop. He ran all day and night. He ordered pizza and ate while he ran. He has since run fifty marathons in fifty states, consecutively. I kid you not.

As a coach, I frequently hear leaders tell me how they don't have time to do this, or they have so much on their plate that they can't do that. Then I remember Dean. Here is a man who had a full-time job, a man with young children in elementary school who made them breakfast every morning and drove them to school each day. Lots of people do that. Except Dean ran a marathon every morning to train for his "ultras." He awoke early, went out for his run, and was back home in time to make his children breakfast and get to work.

It is incredible what people can do when they have passionate desire and determination. You figure out a way. You don't listen to voices that say "No," "You can never do that," or "That is impossible." Instead, you find a way and do it.

Never say never, and don't let others say you can't do it. Nix the Negatives and the Naysayers.

Pessimistic, negative thinking causes complaining, hopelessness, avoidance of risks and challenges, putting down of new ideas by other more optimistic people, resisting change, feeling alone and isolated, feeling useless, blaming others, and self-pity. All of these effects can lead to a stress-filled life, lessened professional and personal growth, and our goals being stifled.

Optimism improves the quality of life by making one happier, content, upbeat, and positive. Cultivating optimism is helping people push out all the negative thoughts from their minds so they can be open to consider alternative options and motivation. Optimism can be gained by the act of intentionally pushing out negative thoughts from your mind so you can stay focused, engaged, and motivated.

> *A pessimist sees the difficulty in every opportunity; an optimist sees the opportunity in every difficulty.*
>
> Winston Churchill

Tips for Success

- Be aware of your words. Include positive language in your communication.
- Notice the words and language other people use.
- Recognize the majority of people can change.
- Become adept at being a better listener. Give people the gift of your attention and allow them to be heard. You don't have to fix them or their problem as they see it. They may simply want an ear, and once they feel heard, they can be more open to listen to you.
- Refrain from giving up on people you perceive to be resistant. Most people can change, although it may take time and skillful coaching. They need a leader with a coaching approach—one who will not avoid resistance.

Summary

Negative people can quickly squash your goals and spread negativity throughout your organization. Understanding how to support and shift negativity, individually and with groups, will help every leader manage resistance to change.

Our spoken and written words convey our ideas, goals, intentions, inspirations, outlooks, thoughts, beliefs, hopes, dreams, and perceptions. One's words are simply a mirror of one's thoughts, a living verbalization of them. They are also key in unlocking resistance to change.

Your skillful ability to Nix the Negatives and Naysayers will help you be a successful CHANGEMASTER. You will develop a better understanding of resistance. You can lead people and groups of people beyond what they consider to be impossible.

Rather than join in with the masses of people who agree change is hard and with resistant people who will never change, a leader with a coaching approach is skilled and willing to confront each resistant person. Doing so will help remove what is blocking progress toward your goals.

5

Gather a Group

Individual commitment to a group effort—that is what makes a team work, a company work, a society work, a civilization work.

Vince Lombardi

When I sat down to begin this chapter, I went to a local coffee shop, sat in the corner near a window and an electrical outlet, and began to write. A few hours later, I began to chuckle to myself. After a few cups of tea, I wanted to visit the restroom. I looked at my large sized laptop and realized I didn't want to unplug it and carry it with me. I hesitated and looked at the table nearby and, for a moment, stopped myself and noticed how I would have preferred to carry my laptop to the ladies room rather than intrude on the woman sitting nearby and request help from a stranger. But here I was writing this chapter about the courage it takes to ask for help! So I smiled to myself and approached her. She was glad to keep an eye on my Mac and when I returned, we had a pleasant chat. The benefits of my asking for help this day were a quicker trip to the ladies room, less risk for my laptop crashing on the floor, and the opportunity for human connection.

It seems the older we get, the more independent we become. We become so accustomed to being a do-it-yourselfer that we neglect to

rely on others. We would rather do it ourselves, in our own time, and in our own way
than ask for help. Asking for help feels like we
are too weak or incapable of doing it ourselves. Asking for help is a big deal and a big
challenge for many of us independent types. I
remember my two-year-old relative who
grabbed a toy from my hand when I attempted
to show her how to use it. She said, "Me do
it." Even a two-year-old embraces a prefer-
ence to do it herself. We teach our kids to be
independent and we think we are providing
an important life lesson. We are.

> *Life takes form as individuals that immediately reach out to create systems of relationships. These individuals and systems arise from two seemingly conflicting forces; the absolute need for individual freedom and the unequivocal need for relationships. Individuals cannot survive alone.*
>
> Margaret J. Wheatley

But then along comes a major goal we want to accomplish. Now
what? When the goal is too big or challenging, or when you are busy
with other priorities, there comes a time when you must Gather a
Group. It can be achieved with greater zest, togetherness, and ease.
There are so many reasons why we need to tap into the help of others.

Why Gather a Group?

Truth is we need each other. We need people who support our goals,
changes, and dreams. We need their energy, inspiration, ideas,
creativity, ongoing encouragement, caring, and concern. The bigger
or more challenging the goal is, the greater the need for others to
pitch in. This is a very important step in creating the change you
want. The fact that we need each other and yet avoid asking others
creates a very personal challenge for many of us.

Together you will accomplish much more than you could as an individual. Together you will find the inspiration you might need to make a
change. It is easy to predict how groups of individuals can support a
common goal. When individuals are doing their part, taking some action
toward the goal, it will be more quickly achieved than going it alone.

We all have a basic human need to connect with others. Remember
the ad campaign "Reach out and touch someone?" Our independent
natures often go into conflict with our need for support. We grow up
learning to be independent and pride ourselves in our ability to do so.
Then along comes a challenging goal. Suppose you want to take a job
in Maui and you need help making this decision. Your Limiting
Thoughts tell you that you are crazy; you will be so far away from
everyone you love. Your closest friends send the same messages. So

what do you do? Do you choose to listen to friends or do you follow your gut? Do you have the stamina and courage to take the leap?

Some people do. Many do not. In situations like this, you evoke the need for support from others, from those who can be neutral, and who can inspire you to make the choice best for you. When you are struggling with a big goal or change, look carefully at the people around you. Identify the ones who can and will support you in making your best choice. Doing so may challenge them to examine their lives. They may or may not be as supportive as you would like.

> *None of us is as smart as all of us.*
>
> *Japanese proverb, also attributed to Kenneth Blanchard*

It may be necessary for you to find a new group—a new community of support—people who already possess the courage and inner stamina to follow their goals and make them come true. How will you go about finding them? Like a snake, you may have to shed your old skin and leave some people behind. Are you ready and willing to do that? Is your goal so compelling that you can let go and pursue the journey?

Gathering a Group will give you added support:

- Bringing more energy and enthusiasm to goals
- Bringing in missing skills
- Bringing in creative ideas and solutions
- Sharing concerns
- Bringing a variety of experiences and knowledge
- Creating a sense of community and belonging
- Engaging in shared, meaningful work
- Sharing accountability
- Divvying up the tasks
- Sharing contribution

An Inspiring Example

I can think of no better example to illustrate the power of gathering a group than the inspiring stories and experiences of Erik Weihenmayer. Erik is known for some amazing accomplishments that would seem incomprehensible to most people. In 2001, he successfully climbed Mount Everest. In 2008, he completed his quest to climb the Seven Summits—the highest mountains on each of the seven continents. That already sounds pretty amazing. But the most amazing aspect of his accomplishments is that Erik is blind.

"There are so many ways to climb a mountain. I think people get trapped into thinking about just one way of doing things," says Erik. Imagine for a moment what it took to complete such feats. In Erik's words, "I would not have been able to achieve these things without an internal vision, without some creativity and persistence and without the ability to build a great team of friends around me" (personal communication, Erik Weihenmayer, September 2011). Erik gathered a group and achieved his dream.

Erik's story doesn't end there. In a town in Tibet, blind children were kept indoors and not allowed or encouraged to venture outside, go to school, or engage with others—they were believed to be possessed by demons. The children were shunned by their parents, scorned by their villages, and rejected by society. They lived in a community without resources to help them or people committed to helping these young people.

Sabriye Tenberken, a blind educator and adventurer who established the first school for the blind in Lhasa, invited Erik to visit their school after learning about his conquest of Everest. She had a burning desire to help the children become empowered to live a full life. Erik arrived in Lhasa and inspired Sabriye and six blind students to let him lead them higher than they had ever been before. She and Erik set out to create a plan and convene a team who would take this group of blind teens who had never experienced the outdoors, on a climb of a 23,000 foot peak near Mount Everest (Tenberken, 2009). Did they do it alone? No way. Could he have done it alone? No. The students succeeded.

> In an environment riddled with pitfalls, roping up with good people is the best chance we have. Imagine your team roped together, building upon each other's strengths, growing day by day. You know if you fall, someone will stop you. If someone else falls, you stop them. People might have different responsibilities, different goals, even motives, but you link together behind one vision. The scope and power of that kind of team is unstoppable. (personal communication, Erik Weihenmayer, 2011)

This story is a wonderful example of the strength of the human spirit—to defy what others might see as impossible, to find a way to reach a meaningful goal rather than give up. It also serves as a powerful story of how the strength of a group of committed individuals can pull together to achieve extraordinary goals.

In 2011, Erik and two others formed the team No Limits and engaged in a demanding and challenging competition on ABC

Television's new reality show *Expedition Impossible*. Twelve teams raced each other for a month, enduring eight to nine hour days of grueling challenges in the deserts of Morocco. All the other competitors were sighted. To watch Erik on this show riding a camel, finding his way through mazes of twisted, windy streets, rappelling, whitewater rafting in treacherous waters, and hiking at a rapid pace was to witness a true American action hero.

I interviewed Erik right after the show's final episode in which Erik and his No Limits team incredibly won second place. He talked about having doubts, hitting brick walls, and needing to stay focused all day, every day. "It comes down to a certain mind-set: do you value the change enough to endure the torture?" he said. He discussed adversity as an energy source. Why not harness it and propel yourself ahead instead of letting it bring you down? We discussed the importance of not just any group of people but ensuring that every person in the group is fulfilling a motivation important to him or her.

These are extreme examples of a man who pursued very challenging goals. Erik persisted through his burning desire to "touch the top" and compete with sighted people, and not allow his lack of sight to be an obstacle. Naysayers might have backed off or never begun. Erik succeeded. He figured out a way to achieve his goal. He never wavered from his burning desire. He found a way to make it happen. Erik knew he needed to rely on other people to help him make this journey. He identified a team of support and resources, and together they achieved the goal. He gathered a group!

We give up on our goals to quickly and too easily. We are far more capable of accomplishing the seemingly impossible than we realize.

Asking for Help

No one accomplishes big goals or makes a major change alone. We need to shed our pride and invite others to help. It is okay to ask for what you need. Some goals can be accomplished alone, but many organizational and individual goals that appear out of reach, are best achieved with the help of others.

> *What separates those who achieve from those who do not is in direct proportion to our ability to ask for help.*
>
> Author unknown

If asking for help feels out of your comfort zone, you can start by examining your own history. Do you have a long-held belief that asking for or needing help is a weakness? Do you need to let go of personal pride?

How to Ask for Help

- Purge your pride.
- Let go of your independent nature.
- Recognize the need for support.
- Recognize you are nurturing new relationships and creating a community.
- Be ultra-enthusiastic about the goal.
- Recognize that asking for help is a strength, not a weakness.
- Be specific. Tell the person exactly what you need.
- Identify like-minded people.

Become more conscious of the people you choose to be surrounded by, work with, or your circle of friends or colleagues. Begin to notice who is in your support system. Where are they? How can you find them if they are not within your reach?

In my coaching practice, I have seen a great deal of sadness when people recognize they may not have others to rely on, others they can ask for help. Perhaps it is true that no one is there to offer support or take on a role in supporting the goal. Maybe your current circle of people would not support your goal. If so, it is time to move on and move out into other circles. You may need to challenge yourself to reach out and connect with others. You can still Gather a Group. How? (See Gather Your Group Tool.) This might require you to change in ways you did not anticipate. You might need to step up to the plate. If you tend to be more of an introvert, you may need to step out of your comfort zone.

When you change or step out toward a challenging goal, your current community may not support you. People in your community might even try to hold you back. They might have a greater need for you to stay in the now than you have for motivation to change. You will have to do your homework and seek a community or like-minded souls who will support you and the changes you want to make.

> Snowflakes are one of nature's most fragile things, but just look at what they can do when they stick together.
>
> Vesta Kelly, Author

A Coaching Approach to Leading Groups: "I Have a Group. Now What?"

One of the many reasons why a coaching approach is effective is that leaders take on a different style when leading groups. A leader-as-coach supports both the individuals and the goal. A coach takes on the role of success partner, helping each team or group participant identify what is needed to achieve the goal and managing obstacles that are bound to arise.

If you are leading a group and are frustrated that people are resistant, it might be time to take a look at your team or potential team. Design your group in advance. Intentionally select the right people. If you have a few naysayers in your existing group, it might be time to meet with each person and determine the source of resistance. Developing a positive, trusting, personal relationship is a helpful strategy.

How to Coach Groups

The first step in bringing a coaching style of leadership to a group is to understand what that means, and how leading a group with a coaching style is different than running a regular meeting. I asked a few superintendents who have been trained in a coaching style of leadership what was different now:

- They listened at a deeper level.
- They asked more challenging questions.
- They expected everyone to take action.
- They held everyone accountable.
- They found more trust, honest discussion and respect.

When coaching groups of people, structuring the coaching group for success in advance will ensure it is successful. In most cases, the leader will have to explain what coaching is and is not, and how this group will differ from former groups that people may have participated in:

- Coaching is not advice giving.
- Coaching is a partnership.
  - Coaching is nonjudgmental.
  - Coaching challenges assumptions and limiting thoughts.
  - Coaching is about discovery.
  - Coaching reveals obstacles and addresses them.
  - Coaching has a bias toward action and results.

As I wander confidently towards the realization of my dreams, I am wondering who will be by me side.

Author unknown

Two Group Coaching Models

There are many ways to integrate a coaching approach style of leadership to group settings. Below are two models that are time-efficient and result focused.

Many People, Common Goal

In this model, a common goal is identified. Each participant contributes toward it through identifying and following through with consistent action steps. Each participant is aware of and supportive of the committed actions of others and contributes by taking his or her own action steps and supporting team members to take their action steps, too.

The coach works with both individuals and the whole group, when time and scheduling allows. The coach can also address team issues and obstacles with everyone. Although the goal is the same, it is likely that each participant will commit to taking different action steps. Everyone hears each other. There is a strong sense of shared commitment.

Suggested group size: four to twelve members

Suggested timeframe: one to two hours for each meeting

For example, suppose your school district has a serious problem it wants to address. One building has had thirteen principals in ten years. A team is formed to develop a strategy to recruit and hire a leader who will stay.

There are eight people in the group. The group agrees to meet bi-weekly for ninety minutes.

With a ninety-minute block of time and eight people in the group, the leader would allot ten minutes of specific coaching time to each person, while the other participants observe and listen. At the end of the ten-minute coaching conversation, the client will have identified one to three action steps he or she will take before meeting again. Everyone hears that person. There will be some time for welcome and wrap-up.

Sample action steps:

- Participant A will interview staff members to determine how the culture in the building has impacted leaders leaving.

- Participant B will explore leadership assessments that might be useful for potential candidates.
- Participant C will research hiring practices.
- Participant D will talk with a search firm.
- . . . and so on.

Notice how each person has a personal set of action steps that differ from others. Yet all focus on the goal and the challenge. The group leader is responsible to hold all members accountable to take their promised action steps.

Many People, Different Goals

In this model, each participant has different goals. In each session, every participant speaks about goals, progress, and challenges. The coach provides feedback and guides the client to next best steps. The process continues until all participants have spoken. If time allows, other participants can contribute their thoughts and feedback, without making suggestions or shifting the conversation to themselves. The coach conducts a ten-minute laser coaching session with each participant, at every session. The leader must pay careful attention to the time to ensure each person has adequate time to speak and to be heard.

Another version of this model is to coach half the group in one session and the other half of the group in the following session. This would allow more individual time for each participant while others observe and listen, and allow more time for members to offer supportive feedback.

Suggested group size: four to six; eight if time is longer

Suggested time: one and a half to two hours

As an example, this group of soon-to-be-retired superintendents has six participants and will meet for ninety minutes, bi-weekly:

- Participant A wants to explore relocating.
- Participant B is considering working in the private sector.
- Participant C wants to start a business.
- Participant D is thinking about teaching in a nearby university.
- . . . and so on.

In the second version, more time is allotted for each person. Each person hears everyone's action steps. Each participant has the support of the coach and the support of the members of the group.

Successful Group Coaching

- Keep the group small to enable each person to have time to speak and for the coach to respond.
- Keep the timeframe to one that ensures people stay engaged.
- Maintain confidentiality.
- Meet with individuals or the group in advance to explain coaching, roles, and responsibilities.
- Ensure participants are eager and willing to engage in a group process.
- Keep your eye on the time. Allow at least ten minutes to coach each participant, more if you encourage others to offer feedback.
- Feedback from others should be offered as insights or observations, not suggestions.
- Participants hold each other accountable for actions, as well as the coach.
- Make sure each participant identifies action steps and that others hear the commitments that person makes.
- Combine group coaching with individual, confidential coaching when time and budget allows.

Benefits of Group Coaching

- Cost-effective
- Time-efficient
- Creates a community of support
- Creates group synergy
- Builds on team strength

Challenges

- Trust
- Confidentiality
- Scheduling
- Commitment
- Requires the coach to have excellent facilitation skills
- Identifying ideal participants
- Mandated participation versus voluntary

A bonus benefit of group coaching is that it enables authentic, trusting relationships and a strong sense of community to be formed.

> *I like to strategically surround myself with good people who make me stronger.*
>
> *Erik Weihenmayer*

It can break down walls of defensiveness and boost the organization's culture.

Tips for Success

- Recognize the human need for meaningful connection, purpose, and support.
- Let go of pride.
- Be willing to ask for help.
- Examine your community of support. Back off from those who are not supportive of your goals. Seek people who support you and the goal.

Summary

If your goal appears out of reach to you right now, take some time now to rethink it. It might be high time to think about who can join you in the cause. Who are the best people to help? Who is not helpful? Are there people you may need to back away from?

In gathering your group to address a personal change, scan your inner circle for the most supportive people to be your sounding board and support system. It is essential that you change your independent mind-set that you don't need other people and that you open up and let them in.

A coaching approach to creating successful change is to motivate and mobilize your group. Keep the goal at the forefront and keep all group members engaged in action toward the achievement of your goal.

6

Emotionally Connect to the Goal

The more intensely we feel about an idea or a goal, the more assuredly the idea, buried deep in our subconscious, will direct us along the path to its fulfillment.

Earl Nightingale,
Motivational Speaker and Author

Imagine that you were just diagnosed with a major heart problem and needed to have heart bypass surgery to save your life. Your lifestyle choices created your seriously unhealthy state and you now have no choice but to subject yourself and your loved ones to this frightening surgery and recovery process.

You would think this illness would cause you to seriously reconsider your lifestyle and make the changes necessary to live a healthier life. You would think it would be a no-brainer to whip yourself into shape and become a healthy person. You would think confronting and surviving this surgery would be the needed catalyst to change your life.

You would be wrong.

It was discovered that 90 percent of heart bypass patients did not change their lifestyle following heart bypass surgery. The fear of dying was insufficient to motivate patients to live a healthier life and therefore, avoid future surgery. Knowing you need to change is not enough. Fear is not what motivates us to change. Dr. Dean Ornish, professor of medicine at the University of California at San Francisco and founder of the Preventative Medicine Research Institute studied heart bypass patients. Ninety percent of patients who were provided with information (only) needed to make change, did not do so. On the other hand, 77 percent of patients who had a team of support and focused on the joy of living instead of the fear of dying were successful in making lifestyle changes that helped them avoid future surgery and live a full life. Ornish said, "We need to bring in the psychological, emotional, and spiritual dimensions that are so often ignored" (quoted in Deutschman, 2005, p. 2).

For a few weeks after a heart attack, patients were scared enough to do whatever their doctors said. But death was just too frightening to think about, so denial would return, and they would go back to their old ways. Patients reverted to their old habits as a day-to-day strategy for coping with their emotional troubles that had not been addressed. "Telling people who are lonely and depressed that they're going to live longer if they quit smoking or change their diet and lifestyle is not that motivating," Ornish says. "Who wants to live longer when you're in chronic emotional pain?"(quoted in Deutschman, 2005, p. 2).

Instead of trying to motivate patients with the fear of dying, Ornish helped them reframe by inspiring a new vision of the joy of living, convincing them they can feel better, not just live longer. That meant enjoying the things that make daily life pleasurable.

> *Joy is a more powerful motivator than fear.*
>
> Dean Ornish, MD

Professor John Kotter hit on a crucial insight. "Behavior change happens mostly by speaking to people's feelings" (quoted in Deutschman, 2005, p. 2). This is true even in organizations that are very focused on analysis and quantitative measurement, even among people who think of themselves as smart in an MBA sense. In highly successful change efforts, people find ways to help others see the problems or solutions in ways that influence emotions, not just thought. Kotter concluded that fostering change in organizations depends overwhelmingly on changing the emotions of individual members.

Dealing productively with emotions is not typically taught in leadership programs. The focus is usually on outer issues, knowledge, and facts. Even when you have all the resources and information needed to make an effective change, if you refrain from addressing people's emotions, you miss an important opportunity to assure change happens and lasts.

Too many leaders and organizations use fear as the motivation to change. We can no longer lead or achieve our goals by threatening people to change. It doesn't work. While few would confess that leadership by fear is their desired method, many use fear as a motivator anyway. Many staff members are in environments where their hearts and heads are clouded by the fear of the following:

- Loss of job
- Loss of face
- Loss of respect
- Loss of competence

If we want to achieve lasting change, we have to stop focusing on fear and start tapping into our emotions. It is important for leaders and individuals attempting a change to recognize that tapping into the positive emotions they will feel when they achieve a challenging goal keeps them connected to the goal and motivated to keep moving when it gets difficult. Emotionally Connecting to the Goal means helping people shift to how they will feel when they accomplish their goal.

As I researched and studied lists of words that describe our emotions, I was struck by how many words on the many published lists I found were negative—far more than those that were positive. In the Tools section is a list of words that inspire emotions. I intentionally avoided listing the negative words, as they will not serve to motivate us toward our challenging goals. We are pretty good at those words. It is high time to identify words that inspire and add them to our daily vocabulary.

Fears often begin to arise when we start to move toward new and challenging goals. Sometimes it happens before we implement our action plan, when we feel overwhelmed by the goal, or sometimes it happens after we start moving forward. When you are guiding yourself or others toward an intimidating goal, Emotionally Connecting to the Goal will remind both you and them to look ahead and muster up the courage and stamina to continue.

How to Create an Emotional Connection to Your Goal

> *Goals are not only absolutely necessary to motivate us. They are essential to really keep us alive.*
>
> Herodotus

Working with emotions might be new turf for many leaders. It might be uncomfortable at first. It might feel awkward to discuss one's deepest emotions and beyond that, to know how to handle them. What do you say? A leader with a coaching approach should become comfortable dealing with real feelings versus avoiding them. You would not focus on the past, or healing old hurts. You would engage in honest, meaningful dialogue with others. You would engage in a real relationship.

Positive thoughts have been linked very strongly to achieving goals. People with a positive attitude strive unwaveringly to achieve their goals. Think about athletes who have achieved a victory. You can be sure they implemented strategies that focus on the desired, end goal. Leaders can inspire others to make this very important shift.

It is important for leaders at the onset of sorting out how to emotionally connect with goals to realize you would not be acting as a therapist. It is okay to listen to emotions without feeling you must get involved in healing them, which would be a therapy role. Instead, you would acknowledge negative emotions and help clients shift to identify the positive emotions they expect to feel when their goal is accomplished. It creates an inner shift from fear to hope. Engage others to move toward positive, happy, empowering healthy feelings—those that will arise when they will successfully achieve the goal.

Based on everything I have observed and experienced in my own organizational work life, it was considered taboo to bring your emotions to work, other than having a pity party with peers at lunchtime. People don't often know what to do when strong emotions surface in the workplace. As a friend, we know to listen and to empathize. As a leader, we are stuck. Perhaps you've had some training in dealing with difficult people or conversations, negative ones. Most people I've known would rather run for the hills than sit down with a staff member who is in an emotional state. Often in coaching conversations, strong emotions arise. Don't be surprised.

Imagine you are the principal of a struggling school. You and the staff have worked very hard to implement many new strategies and you are making progress. It is midyear, and some people seem to be losing steam and momentum. Some people begin to express frustration, resentment, and resistance. What do you do?

In this example, a leader with a coaching approach could implement a process, individually or with groups, to help them uncover feelings and reconnect with the goal. You might use a visualization or walk them toward the future using their imagination to "see" success—to see it specifically and in detail. What are people doing as they hear the latest results of state test scores? They are cheering! They've done it! Now, name how they feel: proud, ecstatic, alive, fulfilled, overjoyed, and so on.

Step 1: Become More Comfortable With Emotions

This may take some doing. How do you handle emotions now, your own and those of people close to you? How might you handle intense emotions coming from staff?

- Recognize that the person mainly wants to be heard. You do not have to jump in to solve a problem or fix it. Listen deeply for fears, doubts and Limiting Thoughts behind the words.
- Acknowledge the feelings.
- Validate the feelings.
- Shift from feeling you need to solve the problem to being a success partner.

When you are struggling to achieve your goal or lasting goal, attach a feeling to the goal. Find a quiet place and some alone time to reflect on the emotions you will feel. List all the feelings you expect to have. These are the motivators for you. They should act as constant reminders for why you are persisting toward this goal and why you would go through the challenge of lasting change at last.

Step 2: Shift From Head to Heart

- Get quiet; find an amenable place for reflection.
- Go inner, to your heart.
- Go outside in nature.
- Be future focused and envision the goal accomplished.

Feel what it is like to arrive, to cross that finish line, to get those great test results, to complete your PhD. Those feelings are the motivation needed to get beyond our current comfort zone, beyond our limiting thoughts, beyond the naysayers who are trying to pull us back. Without this emotional connection, we feel like we are just going through the motions. Emotions connect action with purpose to achieve success. (See also Chapter 2: Have a Higher Purpose and Chapter 9: See Success Smiling.)

Step 3: Name Those Emotions

- Notice and identify your emotions you expect to feel when you arrive at your goal. Write them down.
- Bring those emotions to mind frequently as you move toward the goal.
- Envision the Goal.
- Picture yourself at the end of your change journey. Your goal has been achieved! Engage in a brief meditation. Guide your self or others to imagine the goal accomplished.
- How will I feel when I accomplish it?

_____

_____

_____

Emotional connections are felt with the senses. They emerge from your subconscious mind. Intentionally ignore the logical thinking mind when you are attempting to tap into emotions. Just notice what you feel.

Step 4: Surround Yourself With Encouragement (optional but helpful)

- Some people are helped by keeping a picture or other physical representation of the goal nearby.
- Have the staff members or group select meaningful pictures or objects to symbolize the goal.
- Post pictures and images nearby to inspire people working on the goal.

> The thing to do with feelings is to make it safe to feel all of them.
>
> Robyn Posin

The best times to implement strategies for emotionally connecting to the goal are at the beginning of a goal process and anywhere along the way, when you sense someone giving up, stagnating, or going backwards.

When you need a boost of motivation, that is when to pull this strategy out of your bag of tricks.

Let's look at how this can work. Suppose you are an assistant superintendent working with a new high school principal. Matt wants to be successful, yet he begins to see how this new job has caused a great deal of daily anxiety. He begins to wonder why he took this job and if he will be respected and able to guide the staff to remain passionate about helping students achieve their highest potential. He is starting to dread each day. His days have so many negative thoughts he is losing confidence. Something needs to change or he might not make it.

Since most of Matt's thoughts are negative, they are pulling him down. Thoughts are energy sources, and his negative thoughts cause a rapid lack of confidence. The emotions that are beginning to surface are self-doubt and fear. When I say Emotionally Connect to the Goal, I mean attaching *positive* emotions to the goal. In Matt's scenario, the more time and energy he spends on negative thoughts leading to negative emotions, the worse he feels. He might eventually fail or become physically sick.

Having a coaching conversation with Matt would guide him to do these things:

- Think deeply about the goal
- Remember the Higher Purpose for the goal
- Visualize the goal
- Imagine how he will feel when the goal is completed and successful

This strategy helped Matt stay on track and stay focused on the goal and the positive feelings he will have. As he worked through this challenge, Matt talked about the school's goals: increased graduation rate and increased number of girls in high-level math and science classes. Matt had a true desire to assure students were successful. He began to recognize how he will feel when he succeeds and leads staff members to the results and goals for the school. He began to see more students signing up for challenging classes. He formed new committees to develop strategies for boosting attendance and graduation. He shifted away from fear and fret to being fearless and fulfilled. He began to see the goal as a doable one and began taking different and positive actions. His confidence grew and he completed his first school year successfully.

The Mind, Body, and Goal Connection

The fields of neuroscience and metaphysics have provided insight and information about how and why the connection between emotions and goal achievement leads to success. Numerous studies have repeatedly shown that negative thoughts and negative emotions lead to very real physical effects and often serious, long-term illness. Too much stress, worry, and anxiety can put a strain on your entire system and surely affect the pursuit of your goals. If staff members start to feel too stressed and worried, the goal then becomes a source of anxiety and negative energy. Research has shown that stress, anxiety, nervousness, anger, and brooding can result in a number of very real physical problems, including insomnia, loss of appetite and subsequent loss of weight, shaking, dry mouth, heart palpations, chest pains, headaches, sore muscles, cramps, stomach upset, high blood pressure, sleep apnea, respiratory problems, and a host of other ills. How we manage our emotions is key to how we manage our personal or professional goals. Happier healthier staff will get the job done.

Companies lose billions of dollars due to employees who are ill; the physical effects of negative mental states are a key concern for managers and employers. The cost of ignoring emotions in a change process is steep, in terms of illness, medical cost, and missed opportunities to achieve the goals.

Leaders need to become acutely aware of how to work with the energy source of emotions. You cannot walk away and ignore emotions. You will be a more effective leader when you can manage them, harness them, and channel them to create success.

Let's revisit the client, Margaret, mentioned in Chapter 3. She had a lot of Limiting Thoughts about stepping into the life of a poet. She held herself back for a long time. Once she was ready to take some steps forward many fears arose, particularly around her marriage. Through coaching, she was able to stay the course. Her coach helped her stay focused on how she will feel when she completes, performs, and recites her poetry and publishes a book of her works. She and her coach discussed how she will feel when she hears the impact her writing has on readers, or hears herself on a talk radio show. She began to identify positive and powerful feelings—she felt significant, talented, inspiring to others. Those were very powerful moments that helped her break through the negative self-talk that was within her. She was able to bypass her fear as she kept those positive emotions at the forefront.

There is a difference between intellectually embracing something and emotionally absorbing it. One of the first ways you set yourself up for success is to *believe* wholeheartedly in the goal; the continued belief and ongoing focus serve as a strategy for perseverance to make the goal a reality. There is also a mental and emotional connection between your beliefs, aspirations, and experiences. They can cooperate or they can steal the very joy you seek, not only during your process but after you've achieved what you desired.

Tips for Success

- Just like athletes do, create a detailed image of the goal achieved.
- Focus on the positive feelings that will arise when you complete it.
- Call those feelings to mind when you lose momentum or belief in the goal.

> *By deliberately changing the internal image of reality, people can change the world.*
>
> *Willis Harman,*
> *Social Philosopher*

Summary

When we embark on the journey of transforming or bringing challenging goals to life, we must recognize the importance of emotionally grasping the process in addition to intellectually assessing it. An emotional shift takes longer than the mental one. We must recognize the need to attach positive emotions to our goals, even when they feel scary or too difficult. This is one of many factors that help individuals get past doubt and fear and begin to see possibilities.

Setting high goals is a courageous act. Moving toward them consistently and persistently takes tremendous personal strength and the willingness to be guided by one's emotions. Resistance can be lessened when leaders encourage staff members to stay the course and stay focused on how they will feel when they reach their goal.

This is a very powerful concept. Every leader needs to become more comfortable dealing with emotions and their significance in overcoming resistance to change. In the workplace, it is of utmost importance that leaders become comfortable dealing with their own emotions and those of their employees.

7

Maintain Momentum

Ain't nothin' gonna to break my stride
Nobody's gonna slow me down, oh-no
I got to keep on movin'

Matthew Wilder

"**B**reak my Stride" is a very upbeat and peppy song by Matthew Wilder (1983) from the 1980s. I play it during our training program as motivation for reminding us that we should let nothing stop us from moving forward, from heading in the direction of our goal. Nothing. No matter what comes up, the path to change is always action. The way to achieve our goals, changes, and dreams is by taking consistent, persistent action steps toward them. Sounds easy, doesn't it? Technically, it is easy. All we really have to do is take one step, then another, followed by another, and so on.

We don't reach our goals by talking about them. We don't achieve lasting change by wishing and hoping things will get better or by having countless meetings discussing them. The only path to change is action.

As a leader, you are ultimately responsible for the success of your organization and the goals set forth for others to engage in. You may often feel stuck in knowing what to do and how to interface with staff members, so they are willing to change what they are thinking and doing. This chapter will help you shift from discussion to meaningful action.

The coaching approach yields results because of its built-in processes and expectations for action and results. Making change happen depends on planning and committing to move forward, one step at a time. That is (almost) all it takes.

A coaching style of leadership is one in which leaders seek action. Many people are unaware that the coaching process focuses on action—specific action steps that lead to or make progress toward your goals. Coaching is all about action. Action is how we Maintain Momentum—consistent and persistent steps we take daily, weekly, monthly—that make progress toward the desired goals. As long as there is action, there is progress. Until there is action, it is just talk. It can become easy to stagnate when goals are far-reaching or challenging. A coaching approach does not support stagnation; coaching supports action. Leaders who shift to a coaching style of leadership incorporate the ability to guide every staff member involved in the change toward action. This is how:

- Leaders collaborate to identify action steps.
- Leaders guide conversations toward action.
- Leader and staff members brainstorm possible actions.
- Leader and staff members define a precise timeframe for actions to be taken.
- Leaders hold staff members accountable to take action steps.
- Leaders urge more frequent action.
- Leaders recognize change is individualized for each staff member.
- Leaders recognize each person may have different action steps.

All too often we focus on *planning* for the change, anticipating what we will do in the future, or even the near future. We talk about the changes we want, and too often we spend too much time and energy talking about all the reasons why it is too hard. While it is perfectly okay to plan for change, we must move to action and Maintain Momentum. I don't mean occasional little bitty actions. I mean regular, intentional action on a daily basis.

> The elevator to success is out of order. You'll have to use the stairs . . . one step at a time.
>
> Joe Girard

I recall coaching client Karen, an assistant principal who was so shy and introverted that it led her to feel isolated, detached, and depressed. Although she engaged with others at work, she held back in meetings and in most group situations. In her mind, she felt afraid of saying the wrong thing, and she lacked confidence to speak up. She was more comfortable observing than being a proactive leader. She ached to feel more confident. She was very well aware of this lifelong problem and the negative impact it had on her confidence and her career. Karen was smart and intuitive. When she came to coaching, she felt stuck, but ready to address her problem.

Karen's hard-working nature and other attributes helped her get this new exciting leadership position. Her anxiety grew as she stepped into the new responsibility. She did not anticipate how the new role would challenge her. She needed to tackle her inner obstacle, shyness, and create change from her introverted self to someone who can be more effective in groups, teams, and in leading her school to its future.

Karen's lack of confidence was beginning to hold her back from being a successful leader. She wasn't at risk for losing her job. She wanted to be more effective and less stressed over her perceived lack of ability. She also knew that she was far from ready to advance in her career.

Her shyness also affected her social life. She felt alone and disengaged with people. She came to dread weekends. She wasn't alone because no one called to make a plan. She was alone because she did not initiate contact or plans with others. She was ready to change. As often happens, what holds us back at work likely also holds us back in our personal lives. We cannot separate our work life from our home life. A coaching approach can address both. Karen's unhappiness with this situation caused her to look clearly in the mirror and see that she was the source of the problem. She had to make change but didn't know how to begin. She was ready.

The thought of initiating conversations with someone new did not sit well with Karen. It made her extremely nervous and anxious. Over the course of many years, she developed a real sense of fear being with and among people. On the other hand, she also felt a deep sense of safety in her detached world. Yet her goal was so important to her that she was willing to reconsider her behavior and her perception of herself and address her Limiting Thoughts. She became aware that she was more comfortable working with individuals than groups.

In our coaching, Karen specified her goal of becoming more confident and comfortable with and around people, particularly groups of people and to be more engaged and connected in her professional life and her personal life. Once the goal was established, we developed an initial set of action steps. Together we mapped out a weekly action plan to break out of her safe world.

Karen talked about her upcoming week and things she had to do. We were looking for ways to work on her goal. When and where could she extend herself and connect with people in new ways? The first thing Karen thought of was her weekly manicure appointment. Every week, Karen would go to the salon and never talk to anyone while she was there. When she sat with her hands in the drying machine, she would just talk to herself and hope the time would pass soon. In fact, she often noticed how uncomfortable she felt with other women nearby and no one talking to each other. It never occurred to her to strike up a conversation.

This time was different. Karen was ready to grow. In the first week, she committed to initiate a conversation with two new people at the salon. It was easier than she feared. Karen was delighted to report that she had a much more pleasant time getting her nails done. She felt her energy uplifted by her courage to take the action step and the pleasant result of connection with others! Over the course of the next few months, Karen took these coaching action steps:

- Arranged biweekly small group meetings with staff members to address the school's goals
- Scheduled coffee or lunch meetings at least three times per week to get to know staff members better
- Took initiative to lead discussions at meetings
- Held role-playing group meetings to boost her confidence
- Made at least one social plan in advance by Thursday of each week
- Initiated conversations with two new people per day

In a short time, she began to feel more confident and less isolated. Over time, she began to see herself differently. Slowly but surely, Karen began to boost her confidence as a leader and develop a happier social life. While it may look easy to look at the action steps she took, for fearful Karen, each one of those steps initially caused her to feel anxious. The trick in creating meaningful action steps is to design steps that lead to the goal and tolerate a temporary sense of discomfort by doing those things that scare you. (See Chapter 11: Expect and Welcome Discomfort.) For the person making the change, action may not *feel* easy, at first. There is a felt sense of tension between comfort and the known and the discomfort created by doing something new. Over time, it will become more comfortable and therefore, easier.

Karen made the courageous choice to forego the safety of remaining behind the scenes; she confronted her behavior and grew into her professional role. It was time in her life and her career to deal with this issue or face the possible downfall of her career. She courageously worked at this for several months, until the anxiety lessened and her confidence grew.

Coaching to Action

Maintaining Momentum is a significant and underused strategy for creating change and reaching your goals. Of course, you already know that reaching a goal means doing something in order to get there. We must become more conscious of the need to take consistent, persistent action, and to stay in action, and hold people accountable to take those actions.

Leading a change effort means guiding the organization to achieve its goals. Large group or small, when each person is moving forward, everyone is Maintaining Momentum, and the goal will be reached. This is where the leadership challenge lies. Each person has a personal set of thoughts, beliefs, and experiences related to the change. I strongly suggest that leaders address change efforts to individuals rather than to groups. Telling yourself "they won't change" will never help you achieve your goal. It will keep you stuck and frustrated. Instead, implement a coaching approach and find out what Anne and Stan (and everyone else) think about the change. Change is an individual journey for each person. Each staff member should have a personalized set of actions they will take. These actions may differ from the actions of other members. That's OK; just keep everyone moving forward, one action step at a time.

What actions are Anne and Stan, for example, willing to take? When will they take them, and how often? If you think of your goal on an A–Z continuum, where are Anne and Stan now? As a leader with a coaching approach, have a conversation with Anne and Stan to determine how they perceive the goal and their ability to achieve it. The next best action steps for Anne might be vastly different than for Stan. (See Maintain Momentum Tool.)

Let's look again at Karen. For her, to be at a Z would mean she feels filled with confidence in her leadership role, and she has a satisfying and active social life. Her measures of success are that she no longer considers herself an introvert and she enjoys being in groups of people. Initially she identified herself at C in her professional role and E in her personal life. She had work to do. It would be challenging for anyone to make a quantum leap to E to Z. Realistically, we need to make incremental changes, slow and steady action from wherever we are on the continuum until we ultimately reach our goal at Z.

Maintaining Momentum is about staying in action and working on your goal or change every day. It's about—and I repeat—consistent, persistent action on a regular basis that leads you to achieve the change you seek. Whether you are leading a broad organizational change or a personal one, expecting people to plan for and stay in action is crucial to achieving your goal.

> *The way to get started is to quit talking and begin doing.*
>
> *Walt Disney*

Imagine the power this concept of Maintaining Momentum has for you and your organization! Picture everyone in your organization taking action toward the priority goals on a regular basis.

What actions will you take to make your goal reality?

Resistance Ahead!

This chapter could be summarized in just three words—*stay in action.* Change could be easy except that resistance and fear are predictable companions along the path toward your goals. It is because of resistance that change may appear difficult.

> **Commitment + Action Steps + Managing Resistance = Results**

It is common as we move forward toward our goal, to find many forms of resistance surfacing on the way to the change. Some people resist a goal before they ever get started. Very often, resistance occurs once we get started. For some people, it is those first steps that can bring a paralyzing fear to the surface; for others, it can occur down the road. Resistance to change happens at different times for different people. Change is an individual process for each person. When you pursue any change, be well aware of what change feels like so you can plan for it and move ahead, anyway. Change feels different. Change can feel like anxiety, tension, terror, or a mild sense that

something feels off. Those negative feelings can stop someone, causing resistance to surface.

It is often when the person is in action that he or she meets resistance. Expect it. Plan for it. Welcome it. It we do not confront resistance, manage it, and deal with it, we will stagnate, stay stuck in our
fears, or drift backwards. When we have an unattained goal, a number of resistance factors can arise: fear, self-doubt, and assumptions.
Or the left, logical-thinking brain can stop resistance before it starts.
It might be telling you all the reasons why the goal is impossible to
achieve. If we stay in those thoughts and allow them to take over, we
refuse to move and we get nowhere. That will not lead to the goal,
will it?

Shifting From Discussion to Action

A leader with a coaching approach will steer coaching conversations
toward identifying specific action steps each staff person will take.
You guide the conversation *from* talking about the goal *to* choosing
action steps. It is preferred that the members come up with the actions
they are willing to take, not you. Shifting to action is not about *you*
giving suggestions about what *you* think the others should do. The
next best step is the step they create for themselves. Remember the
action steps will likely differ for each person. Anne might choose to
thoroughly review the support materials that accompany the program.
Stan might choose to implement one of the recommended lessons
tomorrow.

When you engage in a coaching conversation, somewhere by
midpoint or before you end the conversation guide the members
toward action:

- Have they identified what they will do?
- When they will do it?
- How you will know when they have taken the steps?
- How they will handle any resistance that arises?

Request specific steps outlining exactly what members will do
and when they intend to complete the task. It is important to gather
the details. Doing so gains commitment and accountability. Without
a "by when" date there is no real commitment. What you have
instead is the likelihood the action will not be taken. The date can be
flexible; the commitment cannot be.

If and when you hear reluctance, there might be an anticipated barrier. If so, deal with it during the conversation so you can banish it in advance, thereby increasing the likelihood of the person taking the action step.

Certified professional coach Lindsley Silagi was working with Marie Livingston, who was at a low point, feeling overwhelmed and hopelessly disorganized. Marie said having weekly action steps

> put things into perspective for me. I went from inundated by my life to realizing in a very short period of time, one week, I could make real progress toward my goals. My Limiting Thought was I was hopelessly disorganized and never going to get anything accomplished. Once I began taking regular action steps, in a few days some sense of order began to settle in. I was making progress.

Marie also realized that she could remove the negative charge of her old words. She wasn't organizing; she was categorizing. She wasn't getting rid of clutter; she was clearing space. Setting short-term goals, committing to action, and using positive language put Marie back on track with ease.

> *It is even better to act quickly and err than to hesitate until the time of action is past.*
>
> Carl Von Clausewitz

Choosing Courageous Actions

If you have ever worked with a personal trainer or an athletic coach, you know that person pushes you to work harder than you would by yourself. He or she will challenge you to do more, more often. That is what gets results. Small baby steps are progress, but you could grow very old until the change or goal is accomplished.

As you know by now, a coaching style of leadership means encouraging people to take action. Yet you should not hold back from encouraging more, more often. Doing so will speed up success and results. After all, aren't results what you are after? You can provide gentle or not-so-gentle nudging that will encourage someone to make that challenging phone call by tomorrow instead of postponing it until next week. It might be making the promise to go to the gym five times a week for no less than ninety minutes. It might mean adjusting a schedule to make it happen.

We all have the same amount of available time. We all have twenty-four hours a day and seven days in our week. How we choose to use them is up to us. If Dean Karnazes, the "Ultra Marathon Man" can run a marathon every day before breakfast, the people you are having a coaching conversation with can find time to implement their action steps, too. You may have to work with them to carve out exactly when. They may have to reflect on their willingness to take risks, to work harder or longer, to do whatever it takes to achieve the goal. Don't change the goal; change the actions and attitude to arrive at it.

> It's not enough to be busy, so are the ants. The question is: What are we busy about?
>
> Henry David Thoreau

Maintaining Organization Momentum

One person alone will rarely create a movement, a major organizational change. It takes everyone moving forward. This is exactly how Erik climbed Mt. Everest—one step at a time, followed by another step. This is the challenge of leadership. Keeping everyone engaged, in action, passionately committed, and consistently moving ahead requires a number of things:

- A deep understanding of each change strategy in this book
- Open, honest and trusting relationships
- Consistent, persistent action by everyone
- Enthusiasm for the goal

Organizational transformation occurs when everyone is on board and in action toward your goals. Like an orchestral conductor, leaders will ensure that all members are taking their next best step, guiding them through and beyond obstacles that may arise.

Tips for Success

- Expect action, no matter how small.
- Be specific.
- Encourage more, more often.
- Put action steps on your calendar, specifically when the steps will be taken.
- Say *no* to other activities.

- Keep the end goal in mind.
- Keep the Higher Purpose in mind.
- Take something off your plate.
- Plan one to three action steps each week for each goal.
- Be accountable to someone for actions taken.
- Be focused.
- Have a plan in advance to deal with resistance.

> *Action, like a sacrament, is the visible form of an invisible spirit an outward manifestation of an inward power. But as we act, we not only express what is in us and help give shape to the world. We also receive what is outside us and we reshape our inner selves.*
>
> Margaret Wheatley[1]

Summary

There is just no way to avoid the fact—you absolutely must commit to taking action if you are committed to reaching your goals. You must start moving and stay moving. You must Maintain Momentum on a regular basis toward your goal: new actions, different actions, repeated action steps. Just as slow and steady won the race for the tortoise, you too can win your race simply by moving forward one step at a time.

The trick in Maintaining Momentum is to start—just get started and keep going. A small step gets you on your way. It gets the energy flowing in the right direction—forward. Expect resistance to arise at some point for each person. Don't let it stop you or the person you're working with. Create a plan in advance to respond to resistance by planning action steps that directly address it.

It can be easy to feel overwhelmed or intimidated by the challenging goal ahead. Feel free to break it down into achievable stages. Plan for weekly, even daily, action steps. If you are leading a team or a group, expect members to identify the action steps they will take, and check in with them periodically. Hold yourself and others accountable and expect commitments to be honored.

Note

1. Printed with permission from Margaret J. Wheatley, *The True Professional.* Retrieved from http://www.margaretwheatley.com/articles/TheTrueProfessional .pdf

8

Ask How Can I?

I sometimes sit and wonder why
We think of the low instead of the high
We think of the bad instead of the good
We think of the can't instead of the could.

TW Frowein

If a blind man can reach the top of Mount Everest, is *your* goal impossible? As mentioned in Chapter 5, Erik Weihenmayer had to adopt a way of thinking that could enable him to bypass his lack of sight to fulfill his dream of reaching the top. Once he refused to let go the dream and refused to dwell on all the reasons he could not do it, he was wide open to find a way forward.

We must find the way forward no matter what the obstacles are, real or perceived. I love the recent commercial I saw that is part of AT&T's advertising campaign, Rethinking Possible. It shows a spelling bee with an audience of bored-looking children and a panel of frustrated judges. A student comes up to the podium and correctly spells the word *baccalaureate.* The judges look at each other and one announces, "Since this competition has been continuing for forty-eight hours and we have yet to eliminate anyone, it is the decision of this board to declare all twenty contestants winners. You have all competed admirably, *A-D-M-I-R-A-B-L-Y*"(AT&T, 2011).

Traditionally a spelling bee is expected to weed out students and identify the best speller in town or the country. Tension and competition fill the air. In the commercial, everyone seems stunned that so many students are successful. Everyone is a great speller. Everyone wins. And why not? Why do we have to be surprised that everyone can be a winner!

Many Baby Boomers were raised by parents who grew up in and lived through the Great Depression. Life was hard. The culture of the country was survival and struggle. Our parents were grateful to have enough to eat and pay the bills. Few people lived their dreams or even considered that they might be within their reach. Many dreams were lost and never brought to fruition. My mom lived in one-bedroom apartment with her parents and two siblings. Having a goal or a dream was not part of her thinking. It might have been viewed as whimsical so she went through her life without a dream or she learned to squelch them. The focus on getting through each day, the security of having a good job, and being responsible was enough.

It wasn't until the Baby Boomer generation that people started to think about themselves and what they wanted for their lives. It was during the Me Generation that people began to think about what makes them happy.

> *The only way of finding the limits of the possible is by going beyond them into the impossible.*
>
> Arthur C. Clarke, Author

Old ways of thinking often interfere with the accomplishment of a new goal. One must surrender thoughts and beliefs of the past to entertain new ways, alternatives, and possibilities for creating a new future.

Asking "How Can I?" is a creative, courageous strategy, one that involves taking a risk and experiencing the discomfort that accompanies risk. Unless one is willing to consider new possibilities, change will be a challenge. I recall a coaching client who had a burning desire to leave her job and do something more creative. Asking "How can you pursue more creative work?" led her to consider many options. Fearing the financial pinch of leaving her job, we explored other possibilities. She decided to pick up a former hobby of designing mandalas. She began making them late into the night, merely because she loved the process of creating them. She started a blog and connected with others around the world with a similar interest. She not only felt fulfilled and delighted with her sideline, she began to enjoy her "job" much more than she had in the past.

Asking "How Can I?" creates a shift in perception and an opening for moving forward. How one views a goal or change is key to achieving it. Think of a big goal you faced. What were people thinking? What were they feeling? Thoughts and emotions can either energize or drain their energy, toward or away from moving toward it. Asking "How Can I?" opens up possibilities whereas "Why should I?" or "That's too hard or scary" closes down possibilities.

I believe there are always multiple paths to achieve any goal; few goals are truly impossible unless you choose to think so. Therefore, the leader with a coaching approach will guide staff to consider all the possible ways, action steps, strategies, or next steps they can come up with.

Some people were lucky. They had Possibility Thinkers in their life or overcame something that helped them become more positive. If you had parents or other influential adults who did not know how to change and shift from a negative style of thinking to a positive, possibility-thinking style, don't fret. You can start becoming a Possibility Thinker today.

I think one of the major reasons I became attracted to the coaching process, is its ability to break through old thinking and create a world without limits. A coaching approach lets you chip away at real or perceived boundaries and limits. As stated in earlier chapters, most of those boundaries are in your mind. Skilled coaching techniques help you break away from old thinking patterns and the boundaries we have created or those thrust upon us by others. Goals that are not yet achieved often have an underlying cause that people do not believe in the change, or that it is possible to reach it.

Without boundaries we are free to be, do, create, have whatever we wish. We can be open to achieve our potential and bring our dreams to life. We become Possibility Thinkers. We no longer ask, "Why should I?"—we begin to ask "How Can I?" instead.

Leaders of change will be more successful in achieving it when they know how to help people break through negative ways of thinking and become Possibility Thinkers.

Become a Possibility Thinker

Without possibilities we stagnate in yesterday's certainties.

Edward de Bono

One of the ways we become free of Limiting Thoughts is to become a Possibility Thinker. Possibility Thinking is the ability to open one's eyes, bigger, wider, and broader than ever before—to consider new options, to stretch one's thinking, to see with a new set of eyes. Possibility Thinking allows the future to break free from the past by leaving old thoughts behind and entertaining a set of new thoughts that generate excitement and movement.

Take a few moments to think about and identify a big goal, dream, wish, or hope you have had and not yet brought to life.

My dream goal:

_____

_____

_____

Identify your perceived obstacles:

_____

_____

On a scale of one to ten, how important is it to you to fulfill this goal in your lifetime?

_____

_____

_____

Once we begin to adopt a coaching style of leadership and living, we begin to see the negative impact of negative thinking on our goals and dreams. Sometimes we squelch important dreams by letting our Limiting Thoughts and Assumptions take over. Let that way of thinking be in your past. If you want to bring your goal to life, you must let go of perceived limits that have caused you to stagnate or have previously prevented you from moving toward them. Release them.

If you are leading a staff, recognize that individuals have their own sets of Limiting Thoughts, fears, doubts, and former experiences that are blocking them. Possibility Thinking allows for a flow of new outcomes. Possibility Thinking . . .

- Brings new and positive energy to lofty goals.
- Challenges assumptions.
- Needs a burning desire for the goal to be achieved.
- Attracts excitement.
- Increases possibilities for yourself, others, and organizations.
- Allows dreams to come to life.
- Increases the likelihood of reaching your goal.
- Attracts like-minded people to you and expands your support system.
- Gives you permission to dream big.
- Keeps you moving forward.

> I learned the difference between the impossible and the merely never-before done-or-imagined.
>
> George Lucas

As a leader you must help people let go of past Limiting Thoughts, fears, Assumptions— all the negative self-talk that stands between people and their goal. If you would not describe yourself as a Possibility Thinker today, try the strategies in this chapter on yourself first. You will be better equipped to guide others once you begin to be more of a Possibility Thinker yourself.

A recent example with a client allowed her to bring a plan for developing a charter school to life. Prior to our coaching conversations, she let her fears and negative voices rule her and sabotage her progress. She feared leaving a salaried position, yet felt an inner calling to do something else.

How to Develop a Possibility Thinking Mind-Set

It will be mighty difficult to help others become Possibility Thinkers if you are not one yourself. Use the steps below yourself and for the people you are responsible to lead to the successful implementation of an important goal.

- **Think of a big, meaningful goal.** It all starts here, by giving yourself permission to let your big, lofty goal come into the realm of possibility. Never mind that most people think the goal is impossible. Do not let anyone sway you or detour you. What is your greatest hope? What do you want to accomplish in this lifetime? What dreams do you wish you could bring to life? Give yourself or others permission to dream BIG. Take your current dream or goal and kick it up a notch. This is not the time to think small. In this step, imagine there are no boundaries at all. Then dream the big goal. (See the Personal Mission Statement and Higher Purpose Tools.)

• **Image it.** Let your imagination go wild. In your mind's eye, see this goal achieved. See it in vivid detail. What does it specifically look like? Who else can be involved in bringing it to life?

• **Believe it is possible.** Adopt a belief that the goal can be accomplished. It can be done. Anything can be accomplished when we are willing to believe it is so. Let go of Limiting Thoughts.

• **Shift from "Why?" to "Why not?" or "Why should we?" to "How can we?"** Refrain from allowing any negative thoughts to pervade your thinking. What are all the possible ways to make this goal happen? Stretch your mind and include everything and everyone.

• **Focus on the goal not the obstacles.** Don't think about why it can't be done. Shove your left, logical thinking brain out of the way when you are dreaming possibilities. Stay in your right brain, where your hopes, dreams, and heart lie. Stay focused on the goal. (See Chapter 9: See Success Smiling.)

• **Be wildly creative.** Possibility Thinkers are creative. If they do not see a way, they will make one. I remember a motto for a sorority when I was in college, "If I can not find a way, I will make one."

• **Take risks.** Possibility Thinkers are risk takers. It doesn't matter the size of the risk. Just start doing one small thing you might have avoided or resisted before. Volunteer to lead that committee, speak up more often, have that difficult conversation with your boss, and talk to a stranger.

Ask yourself these questions:

What risk have I taken lately?

What can I do today that has an element of risk?

What have I avoided doing that I commit to do now?

• **Be curious.** Possibility Thinkers are curious. They wonder why something has not been done before or how it can be done. They question reality and wonder what alternative viewpoints, strategies, or actions exist to achieve the goal. They are open-minded and willing to consider a new outlook.

• **Step out of your comfort zone, often.** Possibility Thinkers are willing to be uncomfortable. Practice discomfort. Recognize it as a necessity. Celebrate your success by taking bold steps. (See Chapter 11: Expect and Welcome Discomfort.)

• **Focus on how to get there.** Create an action plan and stick to it. Brainstorm any and all possible action steps that you can start doing now. Expand your view. What can you do? Who can come on board and help? Has anyone else ever accomplished a similar goal?

• **Seek positive people: Say No to Naysayers.** Take a hard look at the circle of people in your personal or professional world. Who can support you? Who can join you in this effort? Where can you go to find like-minded people?

• **Spread optimism and enthusiasm like wildfire.** Be a beacon of hope for others. When you passionately believe in the goal, spread it. Do not contain it for fear what others might think. Be an inspiration.

• **Announce your intention.** Tell people about your goal—lots of people. Doing so starts the process. Your goal or dream is no longer on the back burner; it is brought to the forefront. It is no longer a daydream, but a public statement of your goal. I know that can feel intimidating. It's like making a promise. Underneath you may be experiencing fear or anxiety, wondering "Can I do this?" "Can I really pull this off?" "Do I have what it takes?" Acknowledge the anxiety and welcome it as your growth path. Announce the intention anyway. You may be surprised how your enthusiasm and passion for the goal will emanate and attract others to you, who will support you and the goal. Announcing your intention gets the ball rolling. You put out your boundless energy and enthusiasm and you begin to attract people to you who share a similar belief or hope for the goal. Announcing the intention informs and garners others to help you achieve the goal. It states a clear outcome. It shifts the energy from tense fear or intimidation to excitement.

• **Open a Closed Mind.** If you or others are guilty of a closed mind, know it can be opened slowly and steadily by asking questions that challenge your thinking. Ask open-ended questions that cause one to consider other ideas.

• **Watch your Words.** Be mindful of your language. Choose words that uplift, as mentioned in Chapter 6. Pay attention to how you describe the goal to others.

Possibility Thinking sounds like . . .

- "When that budget passes, we can build the science lab we need."
- "Let's discuss how we can accomplish that."
- "In what ways can we get started on that?"
- "Yes, we can!"

Possibility Thinking does NOT sound like . . .

- "The budget will never pass."
- "We'll never find the right person for the job."
- "Been there, done that."
- "That will never work."
- "That can't work."
- "Are you crazy?"

Is Possibility Thinking present in your organization? Begin to notice if it is present or absent. On a scale of one to ten, is Possibility Thinking . . .

- Present in conversations you have or hear? _____
- Part of my leadership communication style? _____
- The norm? _____
- Part of the culture? _____
- Part of how we communicate? _____

What thoughts, words or language need to be dismissed so I can upgrade my communication to encompass Possibility Thinking?

_____

_____

_____

Possibility Thinking challenges us to question our beliefs and consider other perspectives. Old, stale ideas keep us in the past. Fresh, new ideas lead us to the future. Our future depends on those who dare to think beyond the confines of Limited Thoughts.

Possibility Thinking is powered by a new future vision, a burning desire to achieve it and the willingness to tolerate discomfort.

Psychotherapist Saleem Rana (2005) says,"When we surrender our view that we know something, when we are willing to entertain the discomfort of an alternative answer, and when we prefer curiosity to pride, we step into the realm of possibility thinking." Mahatma Gandhi shared the secret to possibility thinking when he said, "If I believe I cannot do something, it makes me incapable of doing it. But when I believe I can, then I acquire the ability to do it, even if I did not have the ability in the beginning."

> *Some men see things as they are and say,"Why?" I dream of things that never were and say,"Why Not?"*
>
> *George Bernard Shaw*

Tips for Success

- Let go of stale, stagnating thoughts.
- Be willing to adopt a new view of the goal.
- Take a risk.

Summary

Remember we can choose our thoughts. Old negative thoughts do not have to be automatic or true. When you let go of old thoughts, you are ready for breakthroughs in how you think, and what you perceive when you change your perspective.

Asking "How Can I?" may conjure up some anxiety. It is to be expected not avoided. Letting yourself imagine possibilities opens a big doorway to creation. Once you begin to consider a possibility previously dismissed, you shift your energy from what might have been stagnant energy to movement. It can take a dormant idea and bring it to life, along with the optimism, motivation, and the uplifting energy required to take action.

> *Much more is possible than people ordinarily think.*
>
> *Benjamin Zander, Conductor and Author*

9

See Success Smiling

Ordinary people believe only in the possible. Extraordinary people visualize not what is possible or probable, but rather what is impossible. By visualizing the impossible, they begin to see it as possible.

Cherie Carter-Scott, Author

Liu Chi Kung was a talented Chinese pianist imprisoned for seven years during the Cultural Revolution. After his release he played the piano better than ever. He didn't have a piano in prison. How could he have improved so much without practicing? "I did practice, every day. I rehearsed every piece I every played, note by note, in my mind" (Zilbergeld & Lazarus, 2008).

Jack Nicklaus says he never hit a golf shot without visualizing the landing down to the blade of grass. Our mind has incredible power over our thoughts, behavior, emotions, and resulting actions. It strongly influences what we see as possible or impossible. Managing our mind is critical to achieving any goal. Leaders need to master skills and strategies to help staff members use their minds more effectively and achieve professional, personal, or organizational goals.

What differentiates people who achieve their challenging goals from those who give up or never reach them? Why do some people appear to be "winners" and leave others behind? The same powerful, peak performance strategies that boost athletic performance and create gold medal winners can be used by every leader and every individual seeking extraordinary success.

Successful people have learned how to incorporate powerful, peak performance strategies that tap into the power of their mind, to create their intended results. This chapter will help every reader develop a rationale for their use and specific how-to techniques. Peak performance strategies are not just for athletes. They can and should be used by leaders, managers, teachers, coaches, and all individuals who have yet to achieve a meaningful goal.

One of the most underutilized strategies for change is the use of imagery or visualization techniques. See Success Smiling incorporates findings from neuroscience and brain function, research studies, and visualization techniques that will help prepare in advance for success. It can be used by leaders to create the future of their organization, and by students who want to achieve their goals. Visualization techniques can help you in your next job interview, presentation, challenging conversation, musical performance, or difficult task. You don't have to be an athlete to use the same mental strategies to master leadership behaviors, student achievement success, or any change you wish.

Mentally rehearsing in advance is how athletes go beyond good to become great. We know that athletes incorporate a whole set of mental strategies to win a race, a medal, or to succeed beyond their last attempt. Olympic running trainer Bobby McGee (personal communication, 2004) reports that 80 percent of the success athletes achieve is through the development of mental strategies, not skill or physical ability. Some sports psychologists report success as 90 percent mental and only 10 percent skill.

The subconscious mind is a powerful tool for achieving anything you want. Peak performance strategies are brain-based techniques that use the power of the mind to bring goals and dreams to fruition. Everyone can learn these. They can be successfully used in any organization or for achieving any goal. Let us borrow what works in athletics and bring visualization techniques to the boardroom and the classroom and achieve similar results.

There are many others who use peak performance techniques:

- Musicians
- Surgeons
- Cancer patients

- Individuals seeking weight loss
- Individuals seeking greater happiness

What the Research Says

There are numerous studies about brain function, neuroscience, Buddhist principles, meditation, and visualization that all support making more regular use of these techniques. Although many people think of them as too new age, scientific evidence supports their use. We can make better and broader use of these techniques and strategies beyond the world of sports psychology.

In the article, *The Effects of Mental Imagery on Athletic Performance,* Annie Plessinger (n.d.) describes many studies of the use of mental imagery. In 1992, Anne Isaac studied the influence of mental practice on sports skills. She divided a group of seventy-eight individuals into a control group and an experimental group. The participants in the experimental group had low to high levels of imaging skills. They practiced trampoline skills for two and a half minutes, followed by five minutes of mental practice, followed by two and a half minutes of physical practice. The control group did math problems and puzzles instead of mental practice. The results of the experiment showed significantly more improvement in the experimental group than in the control group, showing that visual imagery proves effective (Isaac, as cited in Plessinger, n.d.).

Here are results of yet another study. According to Karate of Okinawa (2009), Russia Olympic coaches and scientists set up four training regimens for athletes:

Group 1: 100 percent physical training

Group 2: 75 percent physical training, 25 percent mental training

Group 3: 50 percent physical training, 50 percent mental training

Group 4: 25 percent physical training, 75 percent mental training

Participants in Group 4 showed the greatest level of performance improvement even though they had the least physical training. Athletes in Group 1 performed the worst, although they had the most physical training (Karate of Okinawa as cited in Sisson).

Imagine the results when you apply mental training to your everyday lives and your workplace!

The impact of these studies can have significant effect for organizations, school systems, and anyone interested in achieving anything at a higher level of performance. In schools, educators spend much time, effort, and resources on curriculum, content, and materials. A great deal of energy is spent on "outer" strategies: learning to write, doing mathematics, passing the budget, obtaining the content knowledge we want to cover, and so on. What if teachers and school leaders began to focus more on these peak performance mental success strategies and they could replicate the success of athletes and bring these strategies to the board room, the classroom, the living room?

> *I visualize things in my mind before I have to do them. It's like having a mental workshop.*
>
> Jack Youngblood

Hence, designing programs that combine mental training and rehearsal with physical practice or content knowledge and skill seems to be the method that achieves the best results. Virtually all of the studies show that mental training improves motor skills.

Imagery and Visualization Techniques

Years ago, I worked for Nutri-System, a weight loss program that cleverly used visualization as part of its sales strategy. When people came to inquire about the program, we gave them a tour of the office, weighed them, and took them to our private office for a consultation. We entered their personal data (height, weight, age) into a computer system. The computer would analyze their ideal goal weight and determine a specific date by when they would reach their goal—when they followed the program. The potential clients could "see" themselves successful. We were trained to help them see themselves at their exact by-when date. We helped them identify how they would feel when they achieved their goal, what they were wearing, how they looked and felt. Then we would close the sale.

It was a brilliant methodology for helping people who struggled with achieving this goal to finally "see" themselves achieving it. We would "lead" them to the date in their mind and let them see themselves wearing the size clothes they dreamed about, feeling healthy and confident. All they had to do was follow this plan.

Let us not underestimate the power of the mind to achieve the results we want. It matters not if the goal is physical, athletic, professional, or personal. The same strategies athletes use to bypass average and achieve greatness can be used by anyone to achieve any challenging goal. Sports psychology has long been the home for this knowledge. Using a coaching approach, leaders can bring these strategies to everyone so they can help them reach their goals the same way they help athletes and other performers reach theirs.

> Dream lofty dreams, and as you dream, so shall you become. Your vision is the promise of what you shall at last unveil.
>
> John Ruskin, Author

Peak Performance Strategies

If you were to look for a sports trainer familiar with peak performance strategies, you would quickly notice that they focus on mental preparation, uncovering mental barriers to achieving greatness. Below are commonly used peak performance strategies that help athletes prepare for success:

- Affirmations
- Focus
- Imagery
- Managing anxiety
- Dealing with discomfort

There are several times when it can be especially useful to implement the above steps:

- At the beginning phase of formulating the goal: Sometimes we are unsure what goal to pursue, or we lack the courage to work toward a goal that appears out of our reach.
- On the way: Doubts, fears, and Limiting Thoughts can surface, causing the initiative to slow down, stall, or shift into reverse. When people appear to be losing steam or resistance begins to surface, bring this strategy to mind.
- Every day!

It is not physical strength, skills, or content knowledge that leads us to achieve extreme success. It is the five mental strategies above that keep us going when the going gets rough—that keep us moving, one step at a time, and help us break away from good, good enough, or average to achieve extraordinary.

When you visualize, you rehearse how a problem can be solved, how a new idea could be implemented, or what a piece of art looks like. You see yourself and the goal accomplished. You mentally practice achieving it. If your goal is to deliver an inspiring speech, and the thought of standing before an audience makes your stomach turn, you might develop an image of yourself at the conclusion of the speech. Picture the scenario in detail; see yourself walking to the podium, tall and confident. Picture what you are wearing, the size of the audience, and where you are standing. You see yourself delivering a successful speech. You are finished. You did it. You are getting a standing ovation. The members of the audience have jumped to their feet, feeling so inspired by your words. Pay special attention to how you feel, the joy of success, completion, and accomplishment. See yourself successful—and smile.

How and Why Visualization Is Effective

Among the various ways imagery and visualization are used in sports include mental practice of specific performance skills, improving confidence and positive thinking, problem solving, controlling anxiety, performance review and analysis, preparation for performance, and maintaining mental freshness during injury. The basic techniques are to plan specific mental rehearsals in advance and repeat them often. Memorize them and be ready to use them when needed. It is like creating a movie in your mind and replaying it over and over. Repetition tricks the brain to thinking this act is not new. You have done this before. You can do it. You see yourself doing it and succeeding (more on this later in this chapter).

There are countless techniques for bringing images of our preferred future to mind. Here are some to get started:

- Always begin the process of visualization in a calm state where you feel peaceful. Let go of all distractions, tension, and stress. Take time to become calm before you begin. Focus on right now, the present.
- Conduct a visualization in a location that feels calming. It might mean going out into nature, sitting by a lake, any location that elicits a sense of calm. If you are at home or work, find a quiet spot, play soft music, light some candles, or dim the overhead lights. In my process, I "see" Hanalei Bay in Kauai, one of the most beautiful spots I have ever seen. I see it clearly; I smell the flowers and feel the ocean breeze. I can go there in an instant any time I wish. The more sensory the image, the more effective it is.
- Use all your senses. Describe your surroundings. Create the most detailed image possible of how you achieved and completed your goal. See it in detail; the more detailed it is, the better.

- Visualize yourself smiling. Honor and celebrate your achieve-ment. Adding the smile uplifts your energy and creates a sense of excitement.
- Rehearse every detail, not just the completed act, result, or applause you will receive. See yourself doing each step.
- Rehearse this process often. Have it ready any time you hear someone negate your goal or try to detract you from it. Schedule time to rehearse.
- Notice and direct your thoughts to those that support you in achieving the goal. Immediately squash any negative ones that surface. (Use the Turnaround Statement process in Chapter 3.)
- Create your Academy Award–winning performance. Keep your thoughts focused on achieving the most successful goal or result humanly possible. See yourself (or your organization) receiving accolades for what you have accomplished.
- Identify the specific, positive emotions you feel when you reach your goal and stay connected with them.
- Rehearse your visualization at least two to three times per week.

A Success Story

One of our coaches-in-training, Charles Elbot, principal coach in Denver Public Schools, used a visualization with Jim, an assistant principal, who was struggling with negative rapport with some staff members. Jim believed a few teachers didn't like him. He had little to no communication with some of them for two years. They avoided each other. Jim also thought *they* were the problem. As a result, he carried these thoughts around, which impacted the energy he gave off to others, and felt disappointed with himself and his perceived lack of success. At first, Jim thought there was little he could do to improve the relationships. He thought he was right and they were wrong. One of Jim's goals for coaching was to work on negative relationships that were standing in the way of the school moving forward and of his leadership confidence and success.

One day during their coaching session, Charles asked Jim if he would be willing to engage in a visualization exercise. Then Charles said, "Stand up, feel the floor under your feet, close your eyes, picture the details of your office, hear a knock on the door and see those three to five challenging staff members enter your office. They each offer you a warm smile." Jim envisioned them and saw loving-kindness instead of resentment. He felt an inner shift and sensed that they must like him. They then had a positive interaction. They left the meeting with feelings of warmth and trust.

He stayed in this "meditation" for a few minutes, allowing him the ability to take in the image and how he felt. Charles asked Jim to bring this image to mind every day. Jim did. A few days later, Jim met with Charles and told him that one of the most resistant staff members gave him a Christmas gift and a hug. Later in the week, Jim reported, "I can't believe what happened. It's all different. My relationship with these people has completely shifted. I didn't realize it was all me. I created this." It was Jim who changed. He showed up differently, he perceived the problem differently, and he used the power of his mind to visualize a preferred future. He visualized success smiling!

> *To succeed, we must have a desire so strong that it permeates our subconscious minds.*
>
> David Batchelor

The Science Behind Imagery

Tension and stress repel change. Positive statements, introduced during cycles of slow brain wave activity, accelerate personal change! When we are in a calm state of mind, we shift from the negative, logical-thinking left brain, to our right brain, where our dreams, hopes and emotions lie. We become more heart centered, in touch and in tune with our soul's deepest desires and we are better equipped to squelch resistant thoughts.

The book *Creative Visualization* by Shakti Gawain (1978) describes what happens when you calm yourself. When relaxed, your brain waves slow down. You reach alpha level (versus your waking beta level). Alpha level has been shown to be far more effective than beta level for creating real changes through the use of visualization.

> What this means is that if you learn to relax deeply and do creative visualization, you will be able to make far more effective changes in your life than you will by thinking, worry, planning and trying to manipulate things and people. (p. 11)

Our normal everyday awake state is the beta wave state, where brain frequency is 13 to 30 hertz per second. You are alert and awake; however, you can also be anxious and apprehensive. Meditating or relaxing into a calmer state enables you to enter the alpha wave state.

Patterns of smooth, regular electrical oscillations in the brain occur when an individual is awake and relaxed. Alpha waves have a frequency of 8 to 13 hertz. The more relaxed you are when you use imagery techniques, the more open you are and the more you use your right brain versus your left.

Avoid starting a visualization when you feel tense. Studies conducted by University of Michigan psychologists Rachel and Stephen Kaplan (2009) show that "when you gaze dreamily at drifting clouds, twinkling stars, rippling water, or other natural stimuli, you drift into a soft-focused state that allows your mind to relax and unwind, and lowers your physiological measure of stress" (Kaplan & Kaplan quoted in Gallagher, p. 151). Much of resistance to change stems from allowing our left brain to dominate instead of our right brain, the hemisphere that houses our hope and dreams. Too often people dwell on the left side, especially when a goal seems out of reach. See Success Smiling moves away from the logical thinking, naysaying left brain to the intuitive, hopeful, emotional right brain. Using this strategy, we tap into a brain-based approach to overcoming resistance to change. Becoming more intentional in using visualization techniques will boost enthusiasm to achieve a goal, keep people actively engaged in moving forward, and reduce resistance.

When you visualize, you safely go beyond your comfort zone. You practice executing your steps long before you do them. This sets you (and your brain) up for the real thing. You will develop greater belief in your ability to implement the action steps needed. The more you picture it in your mind, the more likely it is to become reality. Train your brain.

The reason visual imagery works lies in the fact that when you imagine yourself performing to perfection, you are physiologically creating new patterns in your brain, just as if you had physically performed the action. These patterns are similar to small tracks engraved in the brain cells, which can ultimately enable an athlete to perform physical feats by simply mentally practicing the move. Hence, mental imagery is intended to teach our muscles to do exactly what we want them to do (Porter, 1990, p. 17). This is how Liu Chi Kung left prison with a greater ability to play the piano.

Here's how it works. Your left, logical thinking brain looks at the practicality of the goal. That's where those negative voices come from that say "forget it, never happen." Your right brain, your subconscious mind, is where your emotions, hopes, and dreams live. When focusing on a change, you want to intentionally and internally shift, in your brain, from the left to the right side. When you create an image of your goal, you create a picture of what you hope to achieve. You create an imprint of it that becomes stamped in your subconscious mind—your right brain—and held in its memory. The more you focus on it, the more active it becomes.

> *When you visualize, you materialize.*
>
> Dr. Denis Waitley

The mind recalls in pictures. Your subconscious mind doesn't know the difference between an imagined picture and a real one. It assumes the imagined picture is already real.

In an experiment, *The Psychology of Winning* author Dr. Denis Waitley (1995) hooked up Olympic athletes to sophisticated biofeedback equipment and had them run their event *only* in their minds. The same muscles fired in the same sequence when they ran the race in their minds as when they ran it on the track. The mind can't distinguish whether you're really doing it, or whether it's just a practice. Leaders would be wise to incorporate these strategies.

Why Smile?

I read that an American study of four-year-old children and their relationship to smiling showed that children smile about four hundred times a day, while adults smile only fourteen times every day (Thabet, 2011). Smiling has a positive impact. I have found it very valuable to inject a smile during the visioning process. Imagine your very challenging goal ahead. The very thought of it creates tension in your body. Adding a smile helps you experience positive emotions when you think about the goal.

Let's say your goal is to write that book you've been thinking about for years. The process feels overwhelming. So much to do, so little time. You decide to bring this goal to life and this time, you are committed to it. It is still a challenge. You engage in a visualization that will help you imagine your book—finished. It has arrived in your mailbox. You see the cover, with your name, and you are beaming with joy and smiling!

Smiling shifts your energy from anxious and stressful to joyous. Smiling is uplifting. It helps eradicate fear. When you look angry, you spread and communicate negative energy. When you smile, you produce and communicate positive energy, which affects both you and other people positively. A review of 225 studies, involving 275,000 people, authored by Sonja Lyubomirsky, Laura King, and Ed Diener and published in the *Psychological Bulletin* three years ago concluded that happy individuals are more likely to tackle new goals than unhappy people.

Among the benefits of smiling are the following:

- Smiling releases endorphins, natural painkillers, and serotonin. Together these make us feel good. Smiling is a natural drug. Our bodies immediately release endorphins, even when we force it.
- Smiling brings positive energy to the goal.
- Smiling attracts people to us more easily.
- Smiling changes our mood, reduces anxiety, and increases confidence.
- Smiling results in a measurable reduction in blood pressure.
- Smiling improves immune function possibly because you are more relaxed.

> *I just like to smile. Smiling's my favorite.*
>
> Will Ferrell from the movie *Elf*

Why Seeing Success Smiling Works

- You set up your brain for success. You train your brain to be ready for new actions, new goals, and new ideas. When you finally implement the activity, your brain perceives it as already having done it!
- You correlate happiness with the goal.
- You picture yourself successful.
- You plan in advance how you will deal with obstacles.
- You mentally practice each step.

Tips for Success

- Prepare for success in advance.
- Conduct visualization exercises prior to a challenging event.
- Calm yourself before visualizing.
- Rehearse often.

> *Reach high, for stars lie hidden in your soul. Dream deep, for every dream precedes the goal.*
>
> Pamela Vaull Starr,
> Poet and Artist

Summary

See Success Smiling is a tremendously powerful strategy that can be a catalyst for helping your dreams and challenging goals come to life. It can turn around attitudes and help people who might have been naysayers in the past become possibility thinkers today.

When challenging goals seem out of reach or too difficult to accomplish, encourage people to See Success Smiling. Smiling uplifts and affects our heart, happiness, and energy level, propelling us forward. It keeps us emotionally connected to the goal and willing to proceed.

See Success Smiling shifts thoughts to the right brain hemisphere where it sees the "big picture." Focusing on the right brain enables hopes, dreams, wishes, and spontaneity to come to life. We become emotionally connected to our goal by visualizing.

Stress shows on our faces and impacts the people around us. Smiling helps prevent us from looking tired, worn down, and overwhelmed. Smiling can trick your body into changing your mood. When you are stressed, try putting on a smile. There's a good chance you mood will change for the better.

See Success Smiling can be used with individuals or groups. Use it to imagine and bring any goal to life.

10

Turn Talk to the Future

The future never just happened. It was created.

Will and Ariel Durant

"Counting the number of future-oriented sentences in annual reports can predict future innovation," said University of Minnesota marketing professor Rajesh Chandy. "Words, not just actions of the CEO set the tone to inspire, propel and motivate employee innovation," he said. By counting future-focused words and phrases in letters to shareholders, researchers were able to predict the level of innovation by the firm up to five years later (UPI Business News, 2007).

This strategy, Turn Talk to the Future, is about leaving the past behind, suspending challenges of the present, and shifting thoughts to where you and the organization are heading. It's a communication style and skill. In Turn Talk to the Future, leaders shift conversations away from the past and to the goal. We tend to think about "visionary" leadership as those big broad ten-years-from-now goals, and then go about our every day business, making progress where we can. Turn Talk to the Future brings the goal to life on a daily basis. It is a simple skill and strategy that will reap instant rewards. The key understanding in this chapter is to shift away from dwelling on a problem to dwelling on the future, the solution, and the next steps. Leaders must redirect the focus of conversations away from why something is too hard or not possible, toward the creation of the new, of the goal.

There is a plethora of leadership books that can help you create and inspire a vision statement. That is not what I am talking about in this chapter. Turn Talk to the Future is about focusing on the everyday communication and conversation leaders have that will keep that long-term vision alive and engage others in short-term action.

When organizations are struggling to make big changes, it is common for staff members to resist, for people to dwell on all the reasons it is too difficult. You are already well aware of resistance! This strategy will give you a rationale for communicating differently and positively, and keep your eye on the goal. Your job as a leader is to create the future, to execute the action plan to achieve it, and to guide others to come along. Turn Talk to the Future will ease the process.

Recall that each person is a unique individual with personal beliefs, thoughts, interests, values, and dreams. It is necessary for leaders to adopt a new skill set for Turning Talk to the Future—how to live the vision and how to get every person on board.

I remember talking about a challenge with Marty, a high school principal. It was November during a season of serious financial troubles. Textbooks ordered in ample time for the start of the school year had not yet arrived. Everyone was up in arms. Teachers were frustrated, parents were angry, and the principal was on the receiving end of mega-amounts of negativity. Imagine the faculty meetings, the phone calls from parents and students—all venting their frustration on him. While Marty was in no way responsible for this situation, as the leader in this school community he needed to set a tone and effectively deal with the present situation and manage the building full of negativity so learning could occur.

In our coaching sessions, Marty and I talked at length about what was in his control and what was not. Surely uncovering the funds was not in his immediate control. He could not magically produce the textbooks. What was in his control was his attitude, his reactions to others, and his ability to lead people to deal with the situation in a positive manner.

Sometimes we need to vent. Venting is normal, and a release of pent-up negative energy can be healthy. Venting is okay for a little while, but not for too long and not forever. In this situation, Marty began to intentionally focus on the future rather than dwell in the current difficult situation. He began an intentional plan for letting all the people vent, then shifted their conversations to what they can do to make it better. He learned to be a more inspiring leader and helped each teacher focus on what could be done rather than complaining. As a result, there was movement and forward action instead of stagnation. Here's a sample conversation Marty had with one teacher:

Teacher: This is ridiculous. I can't possibly teach without the textbook.

Principal: I hear you and know it is very frustrating.

Teacher: This is a horrible situation. I don't have time to make my own textbook.

Principal: I wish I could produce them for you today. Of course that is impossible. Let's talk about other resources you can use in the meantime. I know how creative you are.

Notice how the principal first acknowledged the problem. Doing so reduced the teacher's defensiveness and created a sense of understanding, empathy, and trust. It is not the leader's fault, yet that person often bears the brunt of the blame. As a leader, it is healthy practice to let go of absorbing blame for a situation out of your control. You cannot control the situation but you can control how you communicate with your staff. You can control yourself, your attitude, and outlook and help each person focus on the future. It takes leadership to keep people moving forward. It takes skill to shift from negativity, fear, doubt, or uncertainty to enthusiasm, willingness, and action.

> *For time and the world do not stand still. Change is the law of life. And those who look only to the past or the present are certain to miss the future.*
>
> John Kennedy

The Future Is Now

Successful visionary leaders know the importance of keeping the organization's preferred future state alive. Successful leaders are charismatic and enthusiastic when addressing the public. They inspire others and help them see the future, the goal down the road, and get excited about it.

When we think of visionary leaders, we often think of a big audience and charismatic and energetic speakers before us. We listen to the future they are speaking about and the picture they are painting. We are inspired by their spoken words and speaking ability. Many leaders, especially middle level leaders, are rarely or ever on the stage, yet they have numerous people reporting to them. They are still responsible for inspiring people to get on the bandwagon and move with the changes the organization needs. We are not usually taught how to inspire, or how to "sell" ideas to others.

Leaders need to take inspiring others further. They need to take this visionary leadership strategy to everyday conversations that leaders have with others. Leaders need to make communicating about the future a daily habit:

- Talk about what you want, where you are going.
- Talk about what you and others can do.
- Talk about how you and others can do it.
- Resist and refrain from allowing conversations to be about endless griping and complaining. You will not get to your goal by dwelling in the past.

Coach Approach

> You are always free to change your mind and choose a different future, or a different past.
>
> Richard Bach, Author

Coaching is a future-focused, action and results-oriented strategy. Turn Talk to the Future is a strategy embedded in the coaching process. By definition, coaching is about creating a preferred future. Leaders with a coaching approach develop skill in moving staff members from discussion to action. They become adept in consciously moving *away* from talking about the problem *to* talking about the result and how they'll reach it. You shift conversations from the past or present situation to the future you are seeking. You constantly and consistently focus on the future. You might talk about why the goal matters, seeking to find meaningful purpose. You talk about how the person can get there. You might break down huge, long-term goals into shorter ones, while always keeping an eye on the longer-term goal. You help people stay connected to it, to stay in action toward it.

Turn Talk to the Future is a small, subtle shift that yields a big impact. It can also lead to a shift in the culture of the organization.

Skillfully shifting away from a problem focus to a solution and future focus creates an atmosphere of hope, of positive energy, and movement.

Talk of the future is just talk if not connected to and followed with action steps everyone in the organization will take. You can easily connect the concepts of this chapter with Chapter 7: Maintain Momentum.

Attributes of a Future-Focused Leader

I would like to add a few essentials to the already known good leadership skills taught in most texts and preparation programs. We already know leaders are successful when they possess strengths in areas as creative problem solving, team building and teamwork, resilience, inspiring, effective communication, and many others. Below are a few more attributes for leaders to become more focused on the future on a daily basis, with everyone.

> *You need people who can walk their companies into the future rather than back them into the future.*
>
> *Warren G. Bennis,*
> *Scholar and Author*

Attributes of a future-focused leader:

- Shifts conversations from past or present to the future
- Curious—is willing to learn how each person views the change
- Uses positive language—is aware of the damaging effect of negative language; uses positive, inspiring words
- Optimistic—sees possibility
- Risk taker—gets out of his or her personal comfort zone; embraces the adventure of change
- Enthusiastic—looks forward to the change
- Flexible—considers alternative solutions or action steps
- Passionate—about the goal
- Maverick—thinks outside the box
- Results oriented—keeps the focus on the goal
- Action oriented—stays in action and expects the same of staff
- Anticipates obstacles and develops solutions in advance
- Encourages creative, innovative ideas
- Decisive
- Motivating—can inspire others

Here's what it might sound like:

Staff member:	"I have so much on my plate. I don't have any time to learn the new curriculum right now."
Leader's response:	"I know you are busy. How can I help you identify a small amount of time this week?"

Self-Talk and Group Talk

Turn Talk to the Future begins with you—your self-talk. Begin to notice how often you dwell on the past, on problems, on feeling frustrated or angry, or any negative feeling. Do you spend most of your energy focusing on the problem or the solution to it? I do not want to deny or ignore problems; surely they exist. Acknowledge what is and move on. Acknowledge that the problem or the challenge exists and swiftly shift to formulating a plan for its solution.

Quantum shift happens when we cease wallowing in problems and negativity. We must be intentional and create the shift. We must deeply listen to the words and language people are using when they talk about the goal. Our words can fuel us and move us forward—or not.

Karen and Barbara teach next door to each other. They never got along and for the most part, avoided each other. They just didn't click. Karen's thoughts about Barbara were, "I don't think Barbara likes me. She avoids me and doesn't share ideas with me." Because Karen felt this way, she created a lack of relationship. She held back. She put no energy into a collegial relationship or a friendship. She created what she thought about. It began to bother her because she felt hurt and rejected. She got along well with most everyone. She wished she had a better relationship with Barbara.

Karen wanted the relationship to shift. We discussed the present state—no relationship, negative feelings. Karen noticed how often feeling rejected bothered her. Sometimes she lay awake at night. In other words, she spent a great deal of time thinking about the problem, too much time.

Karen wanted a better relationship. At the very least, she wanted to feel accepted and have a positive working relationship rather than one of avoidance. Turning Talk to the Future meant shifting away from thinking about how Barbara doesn't like Karen and toward the goal of creating a better relationship with her. Karen's inner thoughts had to change. She began to notice how often she dwelled on hurt and discomfort. Using this strategy, Karen was able to let go of the negative thinking that was draining and hurting her. Instead, she focused on the goal. She thought about a better relationship with Barbara. She visualized a better relationship, let go of negative Limiting Thoughts and took small, regular action steps to improve the relationship.

Focusing on problems deepens the problem. Focusing on solutions creates solutions. Think of a current problem or challenge you have:

_____

_____

_____

How can you shift your thoughts to solutions instead?

_____

_____

_____

Present situations are often a result and reflection of our thoughts. There is nothing productive accomplished by dwelling on problems. If you notice you are guilty of this habit, now is the time to put a stop to it and make the shift to Focus on the Future. Make that a habit and you will more easily and confidently lead others to do so, too. If what you think about you create more of—put more of your thought energy into the future so you can create what you are seeking.

Rationale

While some supporting information about how and why creating what we think works is found in the study of metaphysics, fortunately, neuroscience has also provided the scientific reasons behind how this works and why leaders should pay careful attention to this concept. In a nutshell, we create what we think about. Thoughts become reality. That's right. The more you think about something, the "bigger" it becomes. What you think about, you create. The more you think about something, the more it expands. This is precisely why you want to focus on the solution, not the problem.

You know that saying, "Be careful what you wish for"? Suppose you woke up today and decided you want to buy a yellow Volkswagen. Suddenly you would begin to see them on the road, everywhere. What you pay attention to, your mind responds to by creating it in reality. Your mind will help you find a way. As Mike Dooley (2009) states in his book, *Infinite Possibilities*, "Our words and our actions are merely our thoughts given wings" (p. 7). The term *attention density* was coined by Dr. Jeffrey Schwartz, known for his work with obsessive-compulsive disorder. Attention density refers to the quality and amount of attention paid to a particular mental experience over a specific time. The greater the concentration on a specific idea, the higher the attention density. High attention density facilitates long-term behavioral change (as quoted in Rock, 2006).

What you pay attention to creates physical and chemical changes in the brain. Thoughts reshape your brain pattern. Concentrating attention on a thought, an insight, or a fear will, over time, keep that relevant circuitry open and alive. With enough focus, these circuits become stable, physical links in the brain's structure. This is precisely why we want to keep our focus on thoughts that support the change. The more often we think about them, the more embedded the circuits become. Scientists have been able to track how thoughts move through the brain. We have learned how and why we need to focus on positive thoughts frequently in order to create new mental tapes that become the new (and better) way of thinking.

That is the new way of communicating leaders must embrace. Focusing on a problem makes the problem bigger. Focusing on solutions will lead to creating the solutions. Focusing on fear creates more fear. Focusing on courage creates more of it, and so on.

Let's recall from discussions in earlier chapters:

- Change: It is an individual journey for each person. It is helpful for a leader to discover and uncover each person's next best steps toward the future. No more one-size-fits-all change efforts. Every individual has a personal history and perception and level of readiness to move forward.

- Choice: We all have the power and ability to choose our thoughts. So we must choose to focus on thoughts that support us to achieve our goal, change, or solution and intentionally choose to let go of naysaying thoughts that focus on the problem.

Turning Self-Talk to the Future

In Chapter 2: Awareness of Limiting Thoughts, we focused on how our inner critical thoughts put us down, keeping us trapped within self-imposed boundaries. In this chapter, the emphasis is more on feeding ourselves language that fuels us to achieve our future. So many of the chapters in this book are interrelated and overlap with each other. Turn Talk to the Future is also about Possibility Thinking and Expect and Welcome Discomfort. Nevertheless, in this chapter the focus is on our inner thinking, on our words and patterns of language that support our future creation.

How to Turn Talk to the Future

- Wholeheartedly and passionately believe in your goal.
- Think creatively and boldly.
- Articulate a clear specific picture of the goal complete.
- Listen for words that imply resistance; challenge each one.
- Acknowledge concerns.
- Validate feelings and concerns.
- Use positive, inspiring, future-focused words.
- Shift the conversation from dwelling on the problem to what you can do now to move forward.

Current Thoughts	Future-Focused Response
We don't have time for that project.	What can you do for ten minutes today?
Janet is so negative.	When will you find out why Janet is resistant?

Turning Talk to the Future With Groups

Leaders can generate a great deal more movement and enthusiasm when they change how they communicate with others in group settings. They can truly empower staff members by making a few simple changes in the words and language they use that convey a future focus.

Meredith was leading a biweekly staff meeting in the school district. She was an experienced, respected leader who just obtained a promotion. She possessed good leadership skills, as defined in most textbooks about what it takes to be a good leader. Those good skills didn't help her in a recent staff meeting. Meredith noticed too many people griping about the topic at hand. They were discussing a new reading program the district was implementing. Not everyone was thrilled. There was pervasive negative energy in the room. The meeting wasn't going well. It turned into a battleground.

Meredith had recently completed our coaching skills training. Until now, she used her skills with individuals. Because of the challenging conversations around the table, Meredith applied her new skills in the meeting, and conducted an instant group coaching session. Here's what she did:

- She listened to each person's opinions.
- She acknowledged each person.
- She validated each person's feelings.
- She conveyed no judgment.
- She posed questions that challenged their thinking.
- She kept the conversation focused on the goal for the program and the school.
- She guided the conversation to next-best action steps.

> You can analyze the past but you have to design the future.
>
> Edward de Bono

The tone of the meeting changed. Anger and hostility lessened. There was respectful communication among everyone once Meredith shifted to a coaching style of leadership. People felt heard.

On his web page, language expert Edward de Bono (2000) tells us, "Language is now the biggest barrier to further evolution." He also tells us that "Language is an encyclopedia of ignorance. Words get formed and frozen into permanence at a relative stage of ignorance. That forces us to perceive the world in an old fashioned way." As an innovator in the field of thinking and creativity, de Bono has helped us pay attention to our words, our language and the results we achieve by those we use.

Turning Talk to the Future will challenge you to pay attention to your words and those of others. Use empowering words, positive ones that support the goals—words like *can, when, how, will*—and eliminate such words as *if, try, maybe*. In rapidly changing times, we cannot accurately and precisely predict a future that does not yet exist. We must be open to know it might change along the way. The point is we don't stand still. When we set out toward a large, looming goal, we don't know what will happen along the way, how we and others will feel, what they will do, or if the ultimate goal will change before we arrive. It's OK to move forward with some things unknown. Move forward anyway. Be flexible, open, creative, and continually communicating with a future focus.

> *We have to release the death grip on the past and deal with the future.*
>
> *John Naisbitt, Author*

Tips for Success

- Acknowledge peoples' viewpoints.
- Listen to your spoken words and those of others.
- Use positive, future-focused language.
- Allow a short amount of venting.
- Shift conversations from the past or present to the future.
- Keep the vision and goal alive in words and actions.
- Maintain a solution focus versus a problem focus.
- Take small action steps; they are as important as large ones.

Summary

Creating a new future is a world away from improving the present. Most organizations engage in some form of strategic planning to outline a plan for their desired future. Although we might need more effective planning, we don't really need more of it. We need a new way of executing and communicating how to arrive at the future. Leaders need to understand a coaching approach style of change to master the important skill set for leading each person to the future. It is great to have a charismatic leader to lead the change, but just as important is one with the know-how to take it further, to engage every staff member to embrace the change and move toward it.

What is missing is how. Leaders must move from the dream phase to the doing phase. What does it mean to live your vision on a daily basis? What does it sound like? What do people do in order to get closer? How can leaders communicate with each staff person to carve the pathway to attain it? Today's leaders need a deep understanding and skill set to master the change process. Turning Talk to the Future creates a shift away from problems to solutions.

11

Expect and Welcome Discomfort

Nobody ever died of discomfort, yet living in the name of comfort has killed more ideas, opportunities, actions, and growth than everything else combined.

T. Harv Eker, Motivational Speaker

Six years ago I participated in my first running event and joined a running club to prepare. I was fifty-plus years of age trying to learn to run like an Olympian. No, I wasn't preparing for a marathon—just a 10k race (which felt like a marathon to me). I will never forget a profound comment by my coach, Olympic trainer Bobby McGee. He told us the discomfort associated with our training plan was our learning path. Wow. That was a huge "aha" for me and totally shifted how I perceived the discomfort I was feeling, waking up super-early, pushing myself to run a little more, a little faster each day in the cold and rain. Instead of dreading the discomfort, I listened to my coach's advice and began to welcome it. I realized that discomfort is a necessary aspect of change.

Discomfort is what change feels like! Without it we are likely not trying hard enough, pushing hard enough, doing something new, or thinking differently to affect a meaningful change. There is no getting around the fact that when we attempt something new, it feels different. It is different. It is uncomfortable. That is what change feels like.

Too often we perceive change as too uncomfortable to pursue, so we retreat back to that known comfort. We miss an important point. Because it is right there, in the moment when discomfort arises, that our brain is aware of a change; something new is occurring. We feel it in our breath and our body. It feels like anxiety or stress. Without discomfort there would be no change. Discomfort is not to be dreaded. It is to be welcomed! When you shift how you perceive the stress and anxiety of change, you will have a whole new mind-set and a whole new outlook on change.

Expect that every important change to be made or goal to be achieved will undoubtedly be accompanied by some level of discomfort. It's a given. It is how we perceive that discomfort that challenges us often and derails our change efforts. We run from it instead of embracing it.

Discomfort is physical evidence that change is occurring. It is an alert, a cue. It is something to welcome, as it signals the beginning of change.

As I engaged in my own learning when I became a professional coach, I developed a deep understanding of change and how to master it. I mastered it for myself and with many coaching clients since then. Every yet-to-be-achieved goal requires us to do something different to attain it. We have to step up and do what we have never done before. It is in that doing, taking those new steps, that discomfort arises.

A Personal Example

I used to stop short of trying something new. I would timidly observe others instead of engage. I would admire them from afar and secretly wish I had the courage to do what I feared. I liked my feet on the ground. I remember a beach vacation in Mexico. I was sitting on the sand watching an endless line of people go parasailing. I saw their big smiles when they landed. They seemed to be having the time of their lives. Every morning I told myself I would try it. Every night I felt a nagging sense of disappointment because I chickened out. My fear was too great. I stayed safe, small, and cowardly. I went home without doing it.

Several years later, long after I became a professional coach and adopted a coaching style of living, I used all the strategies found in this book to muster the courage to try parasailing again. This time I was in Hawaii. I received a birthday gift of a parasailing ride. I was still terrified but this time determined.

By intentionally following all the specific CHANGEMASTER strategies in this book, I talked myself through it and bypassed the tremendous sense of discomfort I had. I succeeded this time. Here's what I did:

- **I Challenged my Assumptions.** I assumed I would chicken out again. After all I did before. What must I do differently now? I brought the assumption to mind, and let it go. I said to myself, "Not this time. This time I will prepare myself and commit to do it. I will succeed."

- **I Reflected on my Higher Purpose.** I focused on feelings of pride and accomplishment when I sailed down from above. I thought about how that would carry me forward to overcome other fears.

- **I became conscious of my Limiting Thoughts and banished them.** I noticed my negative thoughts ("I can't do this. I don't have the courage."). Instead I created a new set of thoughts that supported me ("I have what it takes. I can do this. I have a teacher to show me the way.")

- **I Nixed all Negative Thoughts.** I refused to listen to my fears. I sought and talked to people who loved parasailing.

- **I Gathered a Group.** I made sure there were other people aboard the boat. I had a friend with me who was unafraid and understood my deep fear.

- **I Emotionally Connected to the Goal.** I was tired of being a coward and disappointed in myself. I wanted to feel alive. I concentrated on how I would feel when I stepped back into the boat from floating in the air. I thought about the inner pride I would have by overcoming something that was a huge, lifelong fear.

- **I Maintained Momentum.** I stayed in action. I booked the parasailing ride. I arrived early to observe others. I planned for a time-out for myself a few minutes before the ride, to mentally prepare myself.

- **I Asked, How Can I?** I thought deeply about what I could let go of and realized I can do this. I mentally rehearsed all the steps before, during, and after coming down from the parasail ride.

- **I Saw Success Smiling.** This step had a major impact on my ability to complete this goal. In my time-out before the boat left the dock, I meditated and saw myself getting on board, getting ready. I created an image of myself up there, high in the sky, laughing and smiling from ear to ear. I visualized myself returning to the dock, overjoyed at my accomplishment.

- **I Turned Talk to the Future.** Instead of backing off, chickening out, and honoring my fear, I shifted my self-talk from the past to the successful completion of the goal. All my energy and attention were focused on the joyous success I will feel when I told my kids what I accomplished.

- **I Expected and Welcomed Discomfort.** I didn't deny my fear. I acknowledged it and told myself, "I am scared, but I am safe. I am uncomfortable, but I am focusing on the fun instead of the fear." I saw the discomfort from a positive vantage point—one that will help me grow and attempt other courageous acts.

- **I Remained Relentlessly Focused.** This time, I was not leaving my vacation without having accomplished this challenge. Nothing was going to stop me this time. And nothing did.

I needed to bypass my discomfort and fear and step toward a new, exhilarating experience. It didn't matter if my steps were small or large. Because my fear level was high, many of my steps were small. Yours might have differed.

> Death is not the biggest fear we have; our biggest fear is taking the risk to be alive and express what we really are.
>
> Don Miguel Ruiz

Each step in the CHANGEMASTER model was crucial to achieving my goal and feeling super good about it. Truth is, parasailing was easy and fun. Swinging high in the air was peaceful, not fearful. It provided a new view of the harbor, a sense of freedom and accomplishment you can only feel when you do something out of your comfort zone.

This is a highly personal example of how using each of the strategies in this book helped me do something that was previously frightening. Whether your challenge is personal like mine was or professional, use these very same strategies to move past discomfort. The same strategies have been used in work-related settings with clients:

- Prepare for an interview.
- Prepare for a challenging conversation.
- Prepare for a speaking event.
- Launch a new business.
- Write a memoir.

It was my high level of discomfort combined with the unshakable desire to achieve the goal that helped me persist. For every meaningful goal, a certain amount of discomfort will arise. Prepare in advance for it and reframe how it is viewed. Discomfort is normal in a change process. Expect it and welcome it. Welcoming Discomfort creates a path forward instead of something to avoid.

Expecting and Welcoming Discomfort is a game-changer. It is a major shift in thinking that will make a tremendous difference in how you lead and master change. When we are moving toward a brand-new goal or change, we change. We have to. We become different. We become someone who can instead of someone who can't, someone who will instead of won't. We cannot expect to accomplish a challenging change, or even a small one, without some level of discomfort arising.

You can begin by creating a new mental rehearsal that reflects positive thinking. Try it below.

Identify your challenging goal:

_____

_____

_____

How will you reinterpret discomfort? What will you tell yourself to enable you to persist?

_____

_____

_____

Discomfort is a temporary stage. Acknowledge it as proof that you've delved into new territory. Once you do you can begin to welcome it. It is to be celebrated. The challenge of change now begins. Move forward anyway, despite the discomfort. Take tiny steps or quantum leaps. It doesn't really matter how big or small the steps are, just that the steps are forward ones, not backward or stagnant steps.

Leading change becomes doable when leaders guide staff members through discomfort and help them see the positive aspect of it.

Why Discomfort Is Good

Crucial to the success of any change is to understand what is happening, why we feel discomfort, and avoid retreating back to comfort. Discomfort is a signal generated by our brain, sensing something is not right; something feels off. Yes, change does feel

> *We must dare, and dare again, and go on daring.*
>
> *Georges Jacque Danton*

uncomfortable. It is new and new feels weird. When you do something new, your brain notices, and sends you a signal that says, "Something is not right. I am not used to this."

We used to believe the brain stopped growing at a young age. We now know that is not true. Scientists now know the brain can change and form new connections at any time of our lives. When we attempt something new, our brain creates a new connection, a new pathway. With multiple attempts, the newness fades and the brain recognizes the path. Discomfort begins to fade as we integrate the change and when new thoughts and actions become habit.

Try folding your hands the way you normally do. Is your right thumb under or over the left one? Now switch the position of your hands and notice how it feels when you have the other thumb on top. Does it feel comfortable? Normal? Probably not, the first time. It will begin to feel more comfortable over time, with repeated attempts. We lessen discomfort by multiple attempts over time. The brain begins to recognize the new pattern and has been laying down new pathways. As it does, it feels more normal. So we must learn to accept, deal with and Welcome Discomfort as a necessary aspect of change.

When discomfort arises, the signal tells us our brain is doing the work it needs to do to recognize a new activity. The brain needs some repetition of this activity over time. When we observe someone slowing down when he or she is integrating a change, we might interpret it as resistance because that is what we see. Instead, as leaders we need to understand what is going on. Slowing down is to be expected while the brain assimilates the new actions. Slowing down is normal and does not imply resistance. It implies learning and learning takes time. Be patient with the process and yourself as a leader.

On the other side of discomfort awaits courage, trust, exuberance, the thrill of accomplishment, and an abundance of confidence. As one moves toward a change, one moves out of comfort toward discomfort. It starts to show up physically and mentally; the person may feel anxious, nervous, tense as thoughts turn to self-doubt, fear, and uncertainty. In this moment, one has a choice: to move forward and manage the anxiety, to slow down and take small steps, or retreat backward to comfort.

In *Leadership Coaching for Educators* (Reiss, 2007), I identified three stages of change.

- **The Comfort Zone.** This is home base where we feel safe and secure. Energy is neutral.

    In this stage, people feel safe and secure.

- **The Discomfort Zone.** In this stage we feel some level of stress. Change is upon us. It feels different, usually negative. This is where resistance arises and people tend to stagnate or move back to comfort. In this stage, individuals and leaders want to reinterpret the discomfort associated with change, to discovery, enthusiasm, reflection, and willingness to stay the course. Be patient and don't give up. Take small steps if you are experiencing fear. Energy is low as individuals assimilate and process their emotions.

    In this stage, people may feel skeptical, loss, cynical, angry, shocked, doubt, anxious, nervous, unhinged, curious, fearful.

- **The Anything's Possible Zone.** In this stage, individuals realize their goals were doable and feel excited and accomplished. They are ready to take on new goals. Energy is high; doubt and fear are reduced or nixed.

    In this stage, people may feel excited, enthusiastic, hopeful and empowered.

> A dream is your creative vision for your life in the future. You must break out of your current comfort zone and become comfortable with the unfamiliar and the unknown.
>
> Denis Waitley, Author

The best strategy in each stage is to simply keep moving forward. If your goal is meaningful and important to you, don't allow yourself or those you lead to stagnate for too long. Keep the goal in mind and the action plan alive. When strong emotions arise at any stage, be OK with pauses while the person is reflecting, finding meaning in and processing the change—but not forever! Provide empathy, understanding, acknowledgment, and validation of his or her feelings. Encourage the person to take small action steps if doubt or stress is at high levels.

Taking Charge of Discomfort

Change requires a certain amount of courage. We can't be sitting on the sidelines waiting for change to happen. At the onset of a change initiative, you might want to explore your own level of risk taking. When is the last time you did or tried something new? Were you eager, cautious, or hesitant?

> *Every time we choose safety, we reinforce fear.*
>
> *Cheri Huber, Zen Teacher*

It is not unusual for fears to arise when discomfort is high. Fearful thoughts are usually about the future, about something that might happen. Sometimes fears take over and can dominate our thoughts. We might be aware of some of our fears—perhaps we are afraid of public speaking, of financial hardship, or of losing a loved one. Chögyam Trungpa (2010) shows us that most of us suffer from more pervasive fearfulness: fear of ourselves.

> We feel ashamed and embarrassed to look at our feelings or acknowledge our styles of thinking and acting; we don't want to face the reality of our moment-to-moment experience. It is this fear that keeps us trapped in cycles of suffering, despair, and distress. Where does fear come from? It comes from basic bewilderment. Bewilderment comes from being unable to harmonize or synchronize mind and body. (p. 4)

Think of discomfort as a continuum:

---

mild discomfort   →   to   →   paralyzing fear

What does discomfort feel like in your body? Discomfort may feel mild or paralyzing: stress, anger, worry, fear, frustration, anxiety, sadness, depression, rapid breathing, out-of-sorts. When someone is in discomfort, it is helpful for leaders to learn where on the scale from mild to paralyzing someone might be. Fear is the most intense state of discomfort and likely requires a softer, slower approach to change. The more paralyzing the fear, the smaller steps one will be willing to take. In some cases, rest is a meaningful action step.

On the other hand, empowerment also feels different. For some, it can also feel uncomfortable. Empowerment feels positive—a burst of high energy, hope, commitment, joy, uplifting, love, courage, hope, confidence, empathy, compassion. If one has been in a comfortably numb place, even these empowering feelings will feel uncomfortable.

Now let us compare how we feel emotionally and physically when we are in any of such states as dullness, happiness, or joy.

> **emotionally numb to** → **pretty happy to** → **joyful bliss**

Which feelings would you prefer? Which feels better? Which are more likely to help you achieve your goal? All emotions are sources of energy. Happiness uplifts, discomfort drains. We can manage discomfort better when we train ourselves to disengage from the negative feelings and shift toward something, anything, more positive. We lose a lot of energy when we are in discomfort. That energy could be better used for action!

So when discomfort or fear arises, we have work to do. We have to stop and take notice and create a plan to shift from whatever level of discomfort we are in, toward a higher level of happiness, empowerment, and success. How do we do this? We start by accepting the fact that change requires discovery, openness, newness—all feel uncomfortable. Reinterpret discomfort as a growing pain, a necessary and temporary state, until our inner self and habits come to terms with and create new thoughts and new habits. Always move toward joy.

Remember Dean Karnazes (2010), the Ultra Marathon Man from Chapter 4? When asked how he overcomes discomfort he said,

> There's a technique I use I call "baby steps." The first time I ran 200 miles, there was a point where I could not get off the curb. I'd run for 40 hours straight, sat down for the first time and couldn't get up, and thought, "There's no way I'm going to make this 200 miles. I can't even stand up, let alone run another 35 miles." But I just shifted my paradigm. I told myself, "Don't think about 35 miles in front of you. It's too daunting. Just focus on standing up." So I struggled and I

finally just stood up and celebrated the accomplishment. Then I said, "Ok you stood up, now get to the stop sign down the road. Don't think about the 35 miles, just make it to the stop sign and be satisfied." So I got to the stop sign, and said, "Ok just get to the lamppost 100 feet up the road, don't think about what's left in front of you." I did that over and over again and at the end of ten hours, I'd run 35 miles.

Managing Fear

In *Emotional Freedom*, Judith Orloff (2009) says, "Love is the most encompassing force of all, greater than fear, greater than anything" (p. 146). As leaders think about how to move past fear, think about what we are moving to instead—more love, more joy, greater sense of accomplishment, more bliss. Fear is "an

> *Our fears arise from things we don't confront.*
>
> Shakti Gawain

emotional response to danger, perceived or real." Fear is a high form of stress. The upside of fear is that it can save your life. When in danger, your body's warning system notifies and protects you by sending a physical sensation, an alert. If you didn't pay attention to your fear, you could die. There is also a significant downside to fear. It works against you biologically when it becomes a habitual response to everyday conflicts. When people respond to lesser fears the same way they might respond to being in danger, they shut down and can make no movement toward their goal. They are stuck; they stagnate. In such instances we might observe resistance, but we need to recognize they are not in a paralyzing fearful state. They may simply not know how to get out of discomfort. They physically feel the same level of discomfort as if they were in real danger.

As a leader with a coaching approach, you will be able to more effectively lead staff members who might be in varying stages of discomfort, from a real and paralyzing sense of fear to mild discomfort. Simply reinterpreting discomfort as a growing path can be the most helpful influence for you and staff members.

> *You have to leave the city of your comfort and go into the wilderness of your intuition. What you'll discover will be wonderful. What you'll discover is yourself.*
>
> Alan Alda

Managing discomfort can help us reach our goals and help us live a life free of constraints that hold us back. I remember once when my mom spent the night. My son, then a teenager, was out for the evening. He was late coming home.

I watched my mom pace the floor becoming more anxious and worried as the night went on, fearing the worst. Surely if he is late and did not call, something awful must have happened. While this feeling may be easily recognizable by any parent reading this book, the level of worry and pain my mom was in was seriously over-the-top. She was worked up into a fear frenzy and in an awful and unhealthy state of mind. She called the police.

Not long afterwards, my son came home. He was fine. All of that negative energy made her sick and made me angry she was out of control and an unhealthy role model for me. Was I wrong because I didn't buy in to this level of irrational worry? Did I not love my son enough? Of course not. I chose to think he was just late and lost track of time.

> Don't be afraid to go out on a limb. That's where the fruit is.
>
> H. Jackson Brown Jr.

Judith Orloff (2009) tells us:

> The absence of fear is not courage. You are free when you successfully face your fears in a proactive way. Courage requires the presence of adversity. No fear, no courage. Without something to overcome there's no biological push to be brave or conquer negativity, true evolutionary milestones. (p. 146)

Paralyzing fears require a different set of strategies to overcome. For some people and for extreme situations, some form of therapy might be an appropriate approach. I have discovered a number of strategies that help people move away from fear:

- Taking slow, calming breaths
- Meditating
- Visualizing success smiling
- Taking small action steps
- Avoiding negative people
- Exercising
- Focusing on personal growth and courage to face the fear
- Creating positive affirmations
- Appreciating the spiritual meaning of overcoming a challenge

> Fear is a place your soul is stuck and requires compassionate attention.
>
> Judith Orloff

One's past way of responding to fear does not have to be the way for the future. The bonus of embracing courage is the personal pride that occurs when steps past fear are taken. Small steps can yield big results. The positive and empowering feelings that uplift and expand individual's perceptions of themselves or the goal ahead, propels them forward and leads to lasting change.

We must intentionally choose to shift from fear to courage. Since we are in control of our choices, which will you choose—fear or courage? We must be ready or inspired by a goal so meaningful that we will do whatever it takes. I remember the example of Alan, a new high school principal, who had a long-held fear of confrontation. Extremely uncomfortable with arguments, he avoided them whenever he could. An incident occurred in his school that caused an irate parent to schedule a meeting with him. Fortunately, we had a few days to prepare. In this case, Alan focused on a few action steps that helped him ease his fear and conduct a successful conversation. He prepared and rehearsed his thoughts; he and I role-played the conversation. He banished his Limiting Thoughts and created a set of empowering ones and visualized himself confidently concluding the meeting.

Identify something you fear:

_____

_____

_____

Identify one to three steps you will take to move past your fear:

_____

_____

_____

Expecting and Welcoming Discomfort creates an expectation that we no longer will avoid unwanted feelings, but we will take the opportunity to embrace the learning derived from confronting them.

Avoidance is not the path. Courage is. We become more alive, more passionate, and more present when we take a risk and take a step. Courageous leadership demands that you understand what is beneath resistance and provide meaningful support for all staff members, no matter where they are on the discomfort continuum.

I remember talking with a school leader about to start his first superintendency. He came to me for a coaching session to effectively deal with his first media interview. He was raised to abhor the spotlight, to stay away from the limelight. Now, following his goal to be at the helm of a school system, he had to step into roles that were new and extremely uncomfortable.

> *Being on the tightrope is living; everything else is waiting.*
>
> Karl Wallenda

Moving toward a goal challenges us to step up to the plate.

Tips for Success

- View discomfort as a growing pain.
- Recognize that change feels different.
- Notice your emotions; if fear is present, encourage small action steps.

Summary

All change will require feeling different, feeling uncomfortable. Discomfort is nothing more than a symptom that change is occurring. We must learn to reinterpret discomfort typically associated as negative, as a positive instead. We should expect a certain amount of discomfort; without it no real change is taking place. Leaders, as well as anyone wishing to make any type of change, will be more successful with change efforts when they recognize the discomfort as positive. Welcome it.

> *When we're in pain, when we're pushing, when we feel tapped out, we are feeling the most alive.*
>
> Dean Karnazes

12

Remain Relentlessly Focused

Most people have no idea of the giant capacity we can command when we focus all of our resources on mastering a single area of our lives.

Tony Robbins

When is the last time you did one thing at a time? You will probably have to think long and hard about that question. We always feel as though we are doing several things at once, maybe working on your computer and talking on the phone to a parent, or talking to a student while two others are lining up for your attention. It probably won't surprise you that you need to be totally focused on your task so that you will devote the time, emotional, and physical energy needed to achieve it. We have little experience disciplining ourselves to say *no* to other distractions in our lives, or at the office.

Remain Relentlessly Focused is a strategy that will help you say *no* to things that might distract you from the goal, and say *yes* to those things that will help you move toward it. We do a lot of damage when we say yes to absolutely everything, resulting in little time or energy left to work on our goal. It takes a tremendous amount of inner strength and commitment to a goal to master this strategy.

For many of us, our lives are already enormously overloaded and we feel overburdened. When you already have a full plate, how can you possibly add one more thing? Well, truthfully, you can't. Imagine you are on line at a fabulous, gourmet buffet table. Everything looks delicious. You want it all. Half way down the line, you notice your plate can't hold another morsel. As much as you'd love to taste that next yummy looking item, you can't. You either have to take something off (but what?), forego it, or make better choices. You might have to stop and restrategize. You can sit down, eat what you have, then come back. You can choose your most favorite items. You can say no to some items. Then you remember—the diet. Now what will you say yes to, and no to? Every day and every moment is full of choices.

As a coach, I use this strategy to help clients stay focused on their goals, even when other goals, distractions, or demands call for attention. This probably happens to you on a daily basis, on the job and at home. While staying focused may sound simple, in practice it is not. We find it hard to say no and turn someone's request down. We believe we can do it all.

Leaders and individuals who adopt a coaching approach will quickly notice how important and practical this strategy is to task completion and goal attainment. The Remain Relentlessly Focused Tool serves to identify what and when one will do, and not do, each day.

As we became more educated, focusing on our career and family, while raising brilliant children and trying to balance our lives to include some fun, too, we have also become more stressed and less effective. We have less balance in our lives and greater pressure to believe we can do it all. We think we can pull it off and we try so hard to do everything.

Trouble is we really can't. We can't do it all. No, let me rephrase that. We can do it all—just not all at the same time, in the same day, not right now. We have to schedule and plan for our highest priorities and focus on those first, then add others and create time for them.

Narrow the Focus

What is focus? It is defined as "a central point, as of attraction, attention, or activity." You are in focus when you have a high concentration of thoughts and energy toward one thing. Just like listening is intentional versus hearing which is automatic, focus is an intentional act. We have to direct all of our thoughts, energy, and attention toward something.

As you consider the notion of focus, remember the concepts in Turn Talk to the Future and focus on what you want versus what you don't want. Keep thoughts, energy, and attention on the goal, not the problem. As leaders, redirect the focus of conversations and actions away from those that detract from the goal toward those that enable the goal to happen.

One's ability to focus is not a personality trait. It is a discipline, one many of us have lost in our overly busy lives. Stop and think about how many things are typically running through your mind. I believe we have become so used to so much going on around us, so much information overload, juggling priorities at work and home, we have lost the ability to be present and attentive. Even when you know this, it is a challenge to make attentiveness and focus automatic. We have to keep reminding ourselves to narrow our focus, to let go of competing thoughts and concentrate on one action at time.

> *Our thoughts create our reality— where we put our focus is the direction we tend to go.*
>
> Peter McWilliams

Meditation Helps Focus

One of the most common methods for staying focused is the practice of meditation. When your mind is bouncing from thought to thought, always moving and flitting around, it is nearly impossible to pay close attention to something. Time goes by or the day goes by and we feel unaccomplished. For good reason. We have to be able to narrow the focus of our thoughts, actions, and goals, to align them all.

In our hectic, technological world, most of us are constantly connected to cell phones, Blackberries, iPads and the Internet, checking them frequently during the day, or maybe each hour, amplifying the feeling of being pulled in different directions. Learning to meditate can bring us and our priorities back into focus. I witnessed the power of meditating many years ago when I was selling educational products. I had a new product, a set of CDs with calming, meditative music meant to manage disruptive behavior in young children. I had an appointment at the end of a day with a principal in a school for special-needs students. I arrived early and visited with a teacher who was trying to calm her 7-year-old students and prepare them for dismissal. I put the CD in a nearby machine. This was in the 1980s when the concept of meditating and centering oneself was much less mainstream than now. Within minutes, the children were calm. Some actually fell asleep!

Meditating invites us to settle down, to notice and focus on one thought at a time or no thoughts at all. Studies have shown the effects of meditation last beyond the meditation itself. When we meditate, the left prefrontal cortex of the brain—the part of the brain associated with feeling good, and with concentration and planning—becomes more active. Heightened prefrontal activity gives people meditating the ability to intentionally place their attention where they want so they can focus more fully on an image, situation, or task. They are better able to reflect upon and react to situations in a more rational manner.

Meditating enables our brain waves to shift to an alpha-wave state. When in this frequency, we feel calm, present, alert, relaxed, light, and open. This is an optimal state to work on our goals and to Remain Relentlessly Focused. We cannot easily work on them when we are in a state of frenzy. This state can be accessed any time, within seconds:

- Get comfortable.
- Clear your mind.
- Take slow, calming breaths.
- Let go of competing thoughts.
- Notice only the present moment.

Meditating is far from mainstream in organizations. It might feel uncomfortable or unproductive, yet meditating has numerous benefits that can yield greater productivity in the workplace:

- Reduces anxiety
- Increases energy
- Boosts self-confidence
- Supports better focus and concentration
- Increases creativity
- Helps create better relationships
- Increases ability to see the big picture
- Helps one react effectively to stressful events
- Increases job satisfaction
- Deepens understanding

When in alpha, you are alert, awake, and relaxed. As one person reported:

> After a few hours in Alpha some curious and wonderful changes started to happen. My muscle tone softened. I moved with effortless fluidity. Anxiety evaporated. I felt extraordinarily present, centered, posed, open, lighter and freer, calmly energetic and spontaneous. I laughed and smiled more. Untoward events no longer threw me the way they did before. My senses improved. I noticed sounds I hadn't noticed before; and became more aware of the silence. My OCD mellowed. Friends and family responded positively. Everything became easier and more clear than before. (Fehmi & Robins, 2007, p. 31)

Multitasking Is Out: Focus Is In

If you learn nothing else from this chapter, let it be this: Multitasking is out of fashion: focus is in! We've been led to believe we have to become great at multitasking. We are expected to be proud of our ability to multitask and do it well. I bet you have asked, or been asked, in job interviews if you are good at multitasking. To achieve your goal, you no longer want to multitask. You must do the opposite. You must stop doing multiple things at once and start doing only those things that support and serve you in achieving your goal or task of the moment.

Multitasking is not as efficient as we have been led to believe. Instead, become better at focusing on one thing at a time. As we have discovered and learned more about brain function, we now know we can choose the target of our attention and our actions. Therefore, to achieve higher levels of efficiency and greatly increase results, refrain from the temptation to multitask.

Why Stop Multitasking?

To Remain Relentlessly Focused, one must deeply understand why focus and attention are more important than doing two or more things at once. When you try to do two things at once, your attention at any given moment is directed to one or the other activity rather than to both at once. These shifts decrease rather than increase efficiency; they are time and energy depleting. In reality, you are switching back and forth between activities. We are more productive doing one thing versus many. The extra effort makes you less rather than more productive. Your overall performance will be inefficient, error prone and more time-consuming than if you had done one thing at a time.

- Focusing on one activity makes better use of your powerful brain.
- Multitasking reduces your effectiveness in each activity. Switching between activities drains your brain by taking time to shift neural connections.
- More than one activity or switching leads to time-consuming alterations in brain processing and reduces effectiveness.

In her book *Rapt*, Winifred Gallagher (2009) tells us, "Multitasking's most obvious drawback is inefficiency. Your ability to do two things simultaneously is impaired because both tasks draw on one or more of the same information-processing systems in the brain" (p. 8). Our brain is designed to work most efficiently when it works on a single task and for sustained rather than intermittent and alternating periods of time. We can multitask—but we do so at decreased efficiency and accuracy. Multitasking comes at a cost.

According to Jonathan B. Spira (2005), 28 percent of the workday is lost due to interruptions and inefficient ways of working.

> The estimated annual loss to the US economy is said to be $650 billion due to unnecessary interruptions and recovery time. Interruptions consume 28% of the knowledge worker's day. This translates into 28 billion lost man-hours per annum to companies in the United States alone. Assuming an average salary of $21/hour for a knowledge worker, the cost to business is $588 billion.

It would be an understatement to say that attention management—the area of management science dealing with interruptions—merits immediate attention.

The result of Spira's research was staggering—2.1 hours of productivity are lost per knowledge worker per day to unimportant interruptions and distractions and recovery time from interruptions, important or otherwise. Close to a third of the cost of a knowledge worker's salary and benefits is consumed by these unnecessary interruptions.

Researchers Joshua Rubinstein, David Meyer, and Jeffrey Evans (2001) conducted experiments that measured the amount of time lost when young adults repeatedly switched between two tasks. For various types of tasks, valuable time was lost by switching back and forth between activities. If you are working on a spreadsheet, each time you check your email, you lose several tenths of a second. That can add up to a great deal of lost productivity time.

> *When you do not know how to focus your thoughts effectively, they become scattered, miscellaneous, and fixated on "stuff"—negative notions, toxic relationships, and situations from the past.*
>
> Darren L. Johnson

Saying No

Have you ever stopped to realize that when you try and do it all, when you say yes to everything, you feel incredibly drained? Some people can't imagine saying no to their boss or their children. Why is it most of us feel guilty or wrong when we say no? Why is it so much easier for us to say yes to other people's expectations rather than our own? Saying no is an important practice many of us need to learn, not only learn it but resolve that it is okay to do so.

Learning to say no to people and things that detract you from your priorities is an important strategy for everyone. If you are one who struggles to say no, recognize that when you say yes to someone else's request or obligation, you are also saying no to something else. For example, if your boss asks you to work late, you might be saying no to attending your child's soccer game or time you set aside to get to the gym on your way home from work. Time after time, this may happen and eventually cause you to give up on yourself or your goals.

- Saying *No* requires courage.
- Saying *No* honors your values and commitments.
- Saying *No* shows others you stand up for what you believe in.
- Saying *No* communicates your priorities.
- Saying *No* trains others that it's OK to state your boundaries.
- Saying *No* allows you to be clear about your goals.
- Saying *No* earns respect.
- Saying *No* disciplines you to carve out time to focus on your goals.
- Saying *No* creates clear boundaries.

When you say no to what matters less to you, at the same time you saying yes to what matters more. When we do so, we feel stronger, more empowered, capable, and able. You are better able to engage in the creation of your desires, than reacting to the world around you.

Studies about brain function show we can "will" ourselves to do anything we want. We simply have to choose it. We are in control of it all: our thoughts, our choices, our time, our priorities, our values, our actions, and behaviors.

The writing of this book was, for me, an opportunity to practice saying no on a daily basis. It is often a personal challenge to Remain Relentlessly Focused. I have had to discipline myself and find solutions that will enable me to be present and focused on what I want to say in this book. How have I done this? Some days I would unplug my computer from my office and move it to another room. Other days I would go to the "quiet room" in the local library. I even treated myself to a writing retreat for a few days, renting a little condo in the mountains. When our goal is important to us, it must become so much of a priority that we arrange our days to ensure our actions are aligned with our goals.

Just as Saying *No* is important, Saying *Yes* is equally significant:

- Saying *Yes* defines what matters to you.
- Saying *Yes* means you will make time.
- Saying *Yes* honors your commitment.
- Saying *Yes* feels empowering and positive.
- Saying *Yes* communicates your priorities.
- Saying *Yes* takes courage.
- Saying *Yes* can feel fearful.

Letting Go

Sometimes a helpful strategy to increase your focus is Letting Go. Arnie's greatest desire was to become a high school principal. He spent a few months applying and interviewing in various locations. On a lark, he applied for, and was offered, an ideal position in a town three hours away. At first, Arnie had planned to stay local but did not obtain a nearby position.

Often, our goals challenge us to examine our values and beliefs. In this case, Arnie had a great deal to consider: letting go of the comfort of the town he'd lived in for many years, letting go of familiarity, people, his community, and colleagues.

Think of your significant goal or the change you want to make. To achieve it, what might you have to or need to let go of in order to achieve it? What will it take for you to do so? What personal challenges might arise?

Individuals with job performance challenges might need to let go of blaming others or of the way they view themselves. What strategies might you use to let go of something? Sometimes what we have to let go of is something mental, emotional, physical, or spiritual. When we want to make a positive change, it will be helpful to prepare in advance to let go. Here are some examples:

Letting Go of Thoughts

> I'm not sure that will work.

> I never say the right thing.

Letting Go of Feelings

> I am so mad at Amy.

> I'm disappointed with myself.

Letting Go of Something Tangible

> I am willing to sell my house if that is what it takes for me to have the job I want.

Pay Attention to Your Attention

Remain Relentlessly Focused drives home the importance of keeping the priority goal at the forefront and letting go of unrelated distractors. The potential for distraction away from our goals is overwhelming and prevalent in all of our lives. So many things compete for our time and attention—the demands of life, roles, responsibilities, technology, and the constant bombardment of information.

Attention is said to be "the concentration of mental power." What you pay attention to has great influence on what you think, feel, and experience. Neuroscience and behavioral research are beginning to study how we pay attention and how we manage it. Discoveries have revealed that the basic mechanism of attention is a process of selection. What we choose to attend to becomes our reality.

> There is no tidy "attention center" in the brain. Instead an ensemble of alerting, orienting and executive networks collaborate to attend you to what's going on in your inner or

> *The mind has its own place, and in itself can make a heav'n of hell, a hell of heav'n.*
>
> John Milton

outer world in a coherent way that points you toward an appropriate response. (Gallagher, 2009, p. 152**)**

It often seems more of our attention is drawn to negative occurrences than positive ones. However, when we realize we can choose and direct our attention by choosing to focus on one thing over another, we can change our experience and results. When a former client, Joan, was nervous about an upcoming presentation, she shifted her attention away from anxiety to the important information her audience needed; she was more effective and confident.

You have control of what you choose to pay attention to and what you choose to put aside. I like the use of the word *pay* here. If you think about having a limited amount of time, energy, and attention to *spend,* how would you best spend yours to achieve your goal?

How much thought have you given to the style to which you pay attention? Have you stopped to think about your ability to pay more attention to what matters most and less attention to things less important to you? Where is your attention? How many things do you focus on? Are you intensely focused on one thing or is your attention diffused, making it difficult to focus on details?

In the workplace, when our attention is spread across many priorities, it is challenging to accomplish anything at all. Simple tasks might create lethargy and boredom and cause someone to disengage. Difficult tasks might create anxiety and cause someone to shift to something else.

The way you pay attention may or may not be serving you, and may be causing high levels of stress. Your body reacts physically to the way you pay attention. When you shift from intense to diffused attention, your body diffuses stress, normalizing your mental function. Your body ends up in the stable state of homeostasis versus urgency that we feel when attention is intense. Too often, leaders in highly charged turnaround schools or competitive environments feel high levels of stress and become less productive. It is especially important to learn to manage ourselves, our physical self so we can be more attentive, productive, healthier, and happier no matter how challenging our goals or roles are.

> *Energy flows where attention goes.*
>
> Michael Beckwith

Tips for Success

- Function from a calm, centered state; experiment with meditation of other strategy.
- Refrain from multitasking; do one thing, then another.
- Strengthen your ability to say no.
- Identify what you will let go of to make time for change or priority goals.
- Notice how you pay attention.

Summary

It is unnatural to live our lives in a constant state of frenzy. Human beings are designed to be calm, centered, and able to function well. We have lost that. The demands of our outer world have changed us, creating undue pressure and stress that most people think they cannot control. Not true. We are, or should be, in charge of our own central nervous system, not vice versa. We have to take back that control and drive it, and not let it drive us. You can shift back to our natural, centered state. As a leader, you can lower the frenzy level by guiding people to a centered place, by helping them create firm commitments and actions around what is important to do now, and what they can release.

Remain Relentlessly Focused is about being aware of where our focus and attention lie and moving between different levels of attention so we can be more productive with less anxiety. It is a discipline.

13

Conclusion

When I had almost completed writing this book, my friend Gary talked with me about being ready for change in his life, particularly with a budding relationship. I shared the first few strategies with him. A few days later, I was excited to learn how they helped him notice and persist through his Assumptions and Limiting Thoughts that otherwise might have ended the relationship before it had a chance to blossom. His approach, communication, and hope for the future changed as he felt equipped with a new outlook, thoughts, and strategies to propel him forward. I hope yours will too.

After I went through my own personal quest to make some professional and personal changes and become a certified professional coach, I wanted to find a way to communicate to others what I've learned:

- Why all leaders should adopt a coaching style of leadership
- How to simplify the challenge of change for everyone
- Practical strategies for discovering how managing successful change is within reach

I hope by now you too have developed a new attitude about change, are hopeful about your ability to foster it in yourself and others, and see the advantages of adopting a coaching approach to your leadership style. I hope you feel more confident and competent to support people in overcoming resistance to change and create lasting change.

It is important for people referring to coaching that they have an understanding of what coaching is and what it is not. Effective coaching is both a mind-set and a specific skill set.

Underlying Coaching Concepts

- Coaching is nonjudgmental.
- Coaching focuses on the future, not the past.
- Coaching focuses on solutions, not problems.
- Coaching keeps people in motion toward the goals.
- Coaches believe all people have infinite potential.
- People can choose new thoughts and actions at any time.
- Coaches refrain from giving suggestions or advice; rather, they call forth possibilities from the client.
- Coaching differs from mentoring, consulting, facilitating, teaching, or any other helping role.

By adopting the mind-sets and strategies described in this book, you will have adopted a coaching style of leadership. You can use the twelve CHANGEMASTER strategies in any order or for any professional or personal goal. Use them for transforming anything. They are meant to help leaders develop a new attitude and mind-set for approaching change, and a new skill set. Feel free to use them with anyone for any desired goal or change.

> *Leaders today are required to be change leaders. This includes being able to lead personal and individual change for self and others, as well as lead organizational change.*
>
> *John Hefty, retired Executive Director, Colorado Association of School Executives*

As I stated in the Introduction, I wrote this book to inspire people to change their mind-set about change, that change can be easy, and to provide them with strategies to ease on down the typically bumpy road to change.

I welcome hearing from you and discovering how these strategies led you to successful change. Please share your results and stories with me by contacting me at

changemaven@thechangeplace.com

or

www.thechangeplace.com

Challenge Assumptions

Have a Higher Purpose

Awareness of Limiting Thoughts

Nix the Negatives and Naysayers

Gather a Group

Emotionally Connect to the Goal

Maintain Momentum

Ask How Can I?

See Success Smiling

Turn Talk to the Future

Expect and Welcome Discomfort

Remain Relentlessly Focused

CHANGEMASTER Tools

Challenging Assumptions Tool

I have learned as a composer chiefly through my mistakes and pursuits of false assumptions, not by my exposure to fonts of wisdom and knowledge.

Igor Stravinsky

How to Use This Tool

Identify the goal or change.

1. Identify your underlying or hidden assumptions or those prevailing in the minds of your staff members.

2. Determine and decide on one or more strategies to challenge and shift the assumption.

3. Identify new actions to be taken as a result of the strategy. (New actions will help to banish assumptions!)

4. Use individually, or with groups.

Identify the goals or changes you wish to make:

_____

_____

_____

_____

_____

_____

Identify the Assumption	Strategy to Challenge the Assumption	New Thoughts	New Actions
This committee is a waste of my time.	*Find out the plan for following up the committee's decisions.*	*Maybe this time it will be different.*	*I will go to the first meeting now that I see the plan is hopeful.*

Tool.01

Have a Higher Purpose Tool 1

My Joyfinder™

All seasons are beautiful for the person who carries happiness within.

Horace Friess

In this column, list twenty things that bring you joy, in priority order. What do you love to do, see, feel, smell, and so on? What gets your heart pumping and feeds your soul?

Below, list how much time you commit to spend this month on each—and when. Plan at least one per day, and you will find and feel joy each day!

_____   _____

_____   _____

_____   _____

_____   _____

_____   _____

_____   _____

_____   _____

_____   _____

_____   _____

_____   _____

_____   _____

_____   _____

_____   _____

_____   _____

_____   _____

_____   _____

_____   _____

_____   _____

_____   _____

_____   _____

Have a Higher Purpose Tool 2

A Starter Set of Questions

We will be known forever by the tracks we leave.

Native American Proverb

Take sufficient time, in a peaceful place, to ponder these questions:

How do you want to be remembered for your time on earth?

What would you do if you had all the resources in the universe (time, money, support)?

What would you be unstoppable at pursuing your Higher Purpose?

What are you most passionate about?

What might you regret not doing if you neglect it in this lifetime?

What would you be most proud of?

How do you define success?

What are your unfulfilled dreams?

What do you need to let go of to let yourself dream big?

Who do you want to serve? Why?

Have a Higher Purpose Tool 3

Creating a Personal Mission Statement

Don't ask what the world needs. Ask what makes you come alive, and go do it; because what the world needs is people who have come alive.

Howard Thurman

Why Have a Personal Mission Statement?

- ☐ It clarifies the significance for your life and work.
- ☐ It keeps you on track.
- ☐ It provides strength to stand tall in fluctuating winds of change.
- ☐ It helps you be proactive as opposed to reactive.
- ☐ It attracts people that support your mission.
- ☐ It helps focus your energy on what matters.
- ☐ It helps you say *no* to things not aligned with your mission.

Your personal mission statement will be a single sentence that feels empowering when you say it. It should feel strong, inspiring, and energizing. Once you craft it to your satisfaction, write it below; memorize it and recall it when you have challenging choices to make or goals to pursue.

For example, Martin Luther King's Personal Mission Statement was "Equality for all . . . through peaceful means."

Here's how to structure your Personal Mission Statement.

1. What you do (three verbs)
2. For whom (teens, women, etc.)
3. Why (for example, promote world peace)

What I do:

For Whom:

Why:

My Personal Mission Statement

Tool.04

Examining Limiting Thoughts Tool

No pessimist ever discovered the secret of the stars, or sailed to an uncharted land, or opened a new doorway for the human spirit.

Helen Keller

Identifying one's inner thoughts is essential for creating change or achieving a challenging goal. Begin to examine your Limiting Thoughts by noticing those that may be part of your current thinking. Create new thoughts that create the opposite thinking; a Turnaround Statement.

The newly created Turnaround Statement should be positive and create a picture of the preferred future state. It doesn't matter if it doesn't exist yet. Write it in the present tense, as if it is already happening.

Example:

Limiting Thought—I could never be that lucky.

Turnaround Statement—All of my dreams are possible.

Write each Limiting Thought below. Next to it, write a Turnaround Statement that reflects the opposite thinking. Post them around you and repeat them when Limiting Thoughts surface.

Limiting Thought	Turnaround Statement
_____	_____
_____	_____
_____	_____
_____	_____
_____	_____
_____	_____
_____	_____
_____	_____

Nix the Negatives and Naysayers Tool 1

A to Z Uplifting Words

Abundant	Dazzling	Heavenly	Positive	Special
Accomplish	Delight	Helpful	Powerful	Spectacular
Achieve	Discover	Honest	Productive	Spirited
Action	Distinguished	Idea	Prosperous	Splendid
Active	Dynamic	Ideal	Protect	Spontaneous
Admire	Eager	Imaginative	Purpose	Stillness
Adventure	Ease	Increase	Quality	Strong
Affirm	Efficient	Incredible	Quest	Success
Agree	Effortless	Independent	Quick	Sunny
Alive	Encourage	Ingenious	Quiet	Support
Amaze	Energized	Innovate	Recognized	Sure
Appealing	Energy	Inspire	Refresh	Surprise
Appreciate	Enjoy	Instinct	Rejoice	Sustain
Approve	Enthusiastic	Intelligent	Rejuvenate	Terrific
Assertive	Exciting	Inventive	Relax	Thankful
Astounding	Exhilarating	Jovial	Remarkable	Thrilled
Authentic	Expand	Joy	Renew	Thrive
Beaming	Explore	Kind	Resonate	Together
Beautiful	Express	Laugh	Resources	Tranquil
Believe	Fabulous	Leader	Respect	Transform
Benefit	Fantastic	Learn	Restore	Treasure
Bloom	Flourish	Light	Revered	Triumph
Boost	Fortunate	Lively	Revolutionize	Trust
Bountiful	Freedom	Love	Rewarding	Truth
Brave	Fresh	Marvelous	Rich	Ultimate
Breakthrough	Fun	Master	Robust	Unbeatable
Brilliant	Generous	Meaningful	Safe	Upbeat
Calm	Genius	Mission	Secure	Valued
Care	Gentle	Motivate	See	Vibrant
Celebrate	Genuine	Moving	Serene	Victory
Cheer	Give	Nourish	Service	Vision
Choice	Glad	Nurture	Shift	Visualize
Clarity	Glorious	Open	Shine	Vivacious
Clever	Glow	Optimistic	Silence	Welcome
Commend	Grace	Outstanding	Simple	Whole
Confident	Grateful	Paradise	Sincerity	Wholesome
Connected	Grin	Passionate	Smart	Willing
Courageous	Grow	Peace	Smile	Wonderful
Creative	Harmony	Pleasure	Solution	
Cultivate	Healing	Plentiful	Soul	
Curious	Heart	Plenty	Sparkle	

Tool.06

Nix the Negatives and Naysayers Tool 2

Noticing the Negatives

When you are serious about change, you must become acutely aware of who is in your camp, who is not, and how you react to and deal with negativity. This can make or break the likelihood of reaching your goal.

Identify the people who (might) nix your goals.

What conversations will you have with each one to determine the underlying reason for their opinions or negativity?

What will you say to people who nix your ideas? Prepare in advance a statement that is positive, inspiring, and empowering.

Identify people who can support you, your ideas, and your goals.

Which words might you need to eliminate from your vocabulary?

Gather Your Group Tool

Alone we can do so little; together we can do so much.

Helen Keller

My Goal:

_____

_____

_____

Think of all the people in your world of work, if this is a work-related goal, who might support your goal. If this is a personal goal, think of all the people in your life. Below are some questions to help you Gather Your Group.

What is the purpose of the group? What goal or change are we shooting for?

Who can help me or us reach the goal?

What steps will we take to create trust?

How will I muster the courage I might need to ask for help?

Tool.08

How will we hold each other accountable?

How will we support each other?

How will we celebrate each other's success?

What specific support do we each need? From whom?

What exactly will I ask of them?

When you suffer together that is when you make the strongest connections with the people around you.

Erik Weihenmayer

Emotionally Connect to Your Goal Tool 1

It is recommended to complete this tool outdoors in nature or at a location that you find inspiring and peaceful. If you are indoors, choose a quiet place away from distractions. Follow the steps below to Emotionally Connect to Your Goal.

My Goal (see p. 165):

_____

_____

When I think about this goal, I feel _____

Identify the positive emotions you expect to feel when you successfully achieve it.

_____

_____

Identify any obstacles you predict might arise.

_____

_____

- Consciously let go of any perceived obstacles. Imagine them floating away.
- Breathe slowly and calmly until you feel peaceful.
- Visualize your goal again, completed. Focus only on the positive feelings you identified above.
- Record your feelings.

_____

_____

(If the emotion is negative, consciously let it go. Bring the goal back to mind.)

Repeat this process any time you feel resistance or your motivation slipping away.

In a group setting, ask participants to share the emotions they will feel. Record them and use them as reminders when resistance surfaces.

The joy of living is a more powerful motivator than the fear of dying.

Dean Ornish, MD

Emotionally Connect to Your Goal Tool 2

Words That Evoke Positive Emotions

Alive	Giving	Nostalgic	Smart
Amazing	Glad	Nurtured	Soothed
Attract	Gleeful	Open	Special
Avid	Glorious	Optimistic	Spirited
Awesome	Grateful	Overjoyed	Stretched
Awestruck	Great	Passionate	Sunny
Belong	Happy	Peaceful	Super
Blissful	Healthy	Perky	Superior
Bold	Helpful	Playful	Sympathetic
Buoyant	Honored	Positive	Talented
Brave	Hopeful	Powerful	Tender
Bright	Important	Proud	Terrific
Calm	Impressive	Quiet	Thankful
Capable	Innovative	Rapturous	Thoughtful
Carefree	Inspired	Reassured	Thrilled
Caring	Inspiring	Reflective	Tranquil
Cheerful	Intense	Refreshed	Transformed
Clever	Invincible	Rejuvenated	Treasured
Competent	Involved	Relaxed	Trusted
Confident	Jolly	Renewed	Trustworthy
Content	Jovial	Renewed	Unstoppable
Daring	Joy	Replenished	Uplifted
Dedicated	Joyful	Respected	Valued
Delighted	Jubilant	Revitalized	Victorious
Eager	Liberated	Rewarding	Warm
Ecstatic	Light-hearted	Safe	Warmhearted
Elated	Liked	Satisfied	Wealthy
Empathy	Listened to	Secure	Whole
Energized	Lively	Self-assured	Wishful
Enthusiastic	Lovable	Self-reliant	Worldly
Excited	Love	Sensitive	Worthy
Exhilarated	Loving	Sentimental	Youthful
Fantastic	Lucky	Serene	Zest
Fearless	Merry	Serious	
Fulfilled	Moved	Sincere	
Gentle	Needed	Skillful	

Maintain Momentum Tool

The major reason for setting a goal is for what it makes of you to accomplish it. What it makes of you will always be the far greater value than what you get.

Jim Rohn

My Goal:

_____

_____

Where are you now, in relation to your goal? Describe your current state. Then, circle the letter indicating where you are now.

A B C D E F G H I J K L M N O P Q R S T U V W X Y Z

How will I know when I have achieved the goal? Be specific.

What action steps will I take today to make progress toward my goal?

Brainstorm all the possible actions you can think of. Prioritize them. Choose those you will do now, next week, and so on.

What might impede me from taking action?

How might I overcome obstacles that arise?

Apply some courage and consider action steps that are a stretch for you. List them.

What else can you do?

Who will you share your action steps with? Who will hold you accountable?

What strategies will you use to stay committed to implementing them? What might you have to say *no* to?

When will you complete the action steps?

Pray for potatoes, but pick up a hoe.

Anonymous

Ask How Can I?
Becoming a Possibility Thinker Tool

My Goal:

_____

_____

Brainstorm Possibilities

List twenty possible strategies or actions to achieve the goal. Don't stop until you list twenty. Doing so will enable you to stretch your thinking and develop courageous or not-yet-considered steps. Do this alone or with a partner.

1. _____

_____

2. _____

_____

3. _____

_____

4. _____

_____

5. _____

_____

Tool.12

6. _____

_____

7. _____

_____

8. _____

_____

9. _____

_____

10. _____

_____

11. _____

_____

12. _____

_____

13. _____

_____

14. _____

_____

15. _____

_____

16. _____

_____

17. _____

_____

18. _____

_____

19. _____

_____

20. _____

_____

Tool 12

See Success Smiling Tool

What the mind can conceive and believe it can achieve.

Napoleon Hill

My Goal:

_____

_____

List adjectives that describe your goal:

Rewrite your goal statement in specific detail:

How will you calm yourself to achieve alpha wave state? Create a process that works for you. You can breathe slowly while counting down from ten to one, or choose another meditative process.

Where will you go or be when you practice visualization techniques?

Identify the positive thoughts and emotions associated with your goal.

Remember to smile!

Turn Talk to the Future Tool

The only thing we know about the future is that it will be different.

Peter S. Drucker

My Goal:

_____

_____

On a scale of one to ten, how future-focused is your leadership style today?

1　　2　　3　　4　　5　　6　　7　　8　　9　　10

How will you shift to a future-focused style of leadership?

What thoughts do you need to let go of to achieve your future goal?

What words do you need to let go of to achieve the future state?

Tool.14

Expect and Welcome Discomfort Tool

It is not the mountain we conquer but ourselves.

Edmund Hillary

Would you describe yourself as timid or fearless or somewhere in between?

| 1 | 2 | 3 | 4 | 5 | 6 | 7 | 8 | 9 | 10 |

timid   **fearless**

Identify a recent change you made, or something you did or tried for the first time.

What did it feel like? Name the emotions.

Identify a new goal, one that you perceive as a challenge to accomplish.

What number describes your level of excitement and enthusiasm about it?

| 1 | 2 | 3 | 4 | 5 | 6 | 7 | 8 | 9 | 10 |

What number describes your level of fear?

| 1 | 2 | 3 | 4 | 5 | 6 | 7 | 8 | 9 | 10 |

What courageous action(s) are you willing to take this week toward this goal? List one to three actions.

1.

2.

3.

What will you do to upgrade your courage level? List one to three specific actions steps you will take this week.

1.

2.

3.

Tool.15

Remain Relentlessly Focused Tool

Energy and persistence conquer all things.

Benjamin Franklin

My Goal:

_____

_____

How much time will I devote to it today? Exactly when?

What actions will I say *yes* to today so I can take action on my goal?

What will I say *no* to today so I can take action on my goal?

How will I bypass detractors that may arise? What will I say to myself or to others?

Be a CHANGEMASTER Tool

How wonderful it is that nobody need wait a single moment before starting to improve the world.

Anne Frank

Below are all twelve strategies. Feel free to copy and use this tool yourself or with staff members.

My Goal:

_____

_____

#1 Challenge Assumptions
Think of the change you identified. What assumptions do you or others have?

#2 Have a Higher Purpose
What is your higher purpose for this goal?

#3 Awareness of Limiting Thoughts
What Limiting Thoughts stop you? Write them down. List your Turnaround Statement.

#4 Nix the Negatives and Naysayers
Identify people who drain your energy and distance yourself from them. Reflect on negative comments you hear and develop your strategy for handling them.

#5 Gather a Group
Who can support you in accomplishing the change?

#6 Emotionally Connect to the Goal
Write down the emotions that you will feel when you successfully complete the goal.

#7 Maintain Momentum
What steps will you take today to make your change happen?

#8 Ask How Can I?
What possibilities exist?

#9 See Success Smiling

What does your change or goal look like? Describe it in vivid detail. Add a smile.

#10 Turn Talk to the Future

How will you rephrase what you wish to communicate so it remains focused on the future?

#11 Expect and Welcome Discomfort

How will you reinterpret discomfort? What words will you feed yourself now?

#12 Remain Relentlessly Focused

What will you say no to so you can free your time and energy for your priority goal?

References

Amen, D. G. (2008). *Magnificent mind at any age.* New York, NY: Harmony Books.

Anything Research. (2011). *2011 industry statistics: Professional and management development training.* Retrieved from http://www.anythingresearch

AT&T. (2010). *Rethink possible.* Retrieved from http://www.youtube.com/watch?v=LCcc8vMSv4w

Begley, S. (2007). *Train your mind, change your brain.* New York, NY: Ballantine Books. Abstract retrieved from http://www.worldcat.org/title/train-your-mind-change-your-brain-how-a-new-science-reveals-our-extra ordinary-potential-to-transform-ourselves/oclc/690284460&refer=brief_results

Chicago Lakes Football: Team + attitude + effort = success. (n.d.). Retrieved from http://www.clfootball.com/playersexpectations.htm

De Bono, E. (2000). *de Bono code.* Retrieved from http://www.edwdebono.com/msg06t.htm

Deutschman, A. (2005, May 1). Change or die. *Fast Company Magazine, 94.* Retrieved from http://www.fastcompany.com/94/open_change-or-die.html

Diaz, J., & Chenetz, R. (2010). *Utter endurance: Iceman and ultra marathon man.* Retrieved from http://abcnews.go.com/2020/iceman-marathon-man-feats-human-endurance/story?id=10731229&page=4

Dooley, M. (2009). *Infinite possibilities.* New York: Atria Books.

Dychtwald, K., & Kadlec, J. (2009). *With purpose.* New York, NY: HarperCollins.

Dye, L. (2011). *Can you smile your way to success?* Retrieved from http://abcnews.go.com/Technology/DyeHard/story?id=6285001&page=1

Ericsson, K. A., Krampe, R. T., & Tesch-Romer, C. (1993). The role of deliberate practice in the acquisition of expert performance. *Psychological Review, 100*(3), 363–406.

Ericsson, K. A., Prietula, M. J., & Cokely, E. T. (2007). *The making of an expert.* Retrieved from http://hbr.org/2007/07/the-making-of-an-expert

Fehmi, L., & Robins, J. (2007). *The open focus brain.* Boston, MA: Trumpter Books.

Gallagher, W. (2009). *Rapt.* New York, NY: Penguin Press.

Gawain, S. (1978). *Creative visualization.* New York, NY: Bantam Books.

George, B. (2007). *True north.* Hoboken, NJ: Wiley.

Graci, S. (2005). *The path to phenomenal health.* Hoboken, NJ: Wiley.

Hoagland-Smith, L. (2006). *Business coaching, corporate coaching, or executive coaching is all about results.* Retrieved from http://ezinearticles.com/?Business-Coaching-Corporate-Coaching-or-Executive-Coaching-is-All-About-Results&id=389291

International Coach Federation. (2009). *Global coaching client study.* Retrieved from http://www.coachfederation.org

Iyengar, S. (2010). *The art of choosing.* New York, NY: Twelve.

Janis, I. L. (1982). *Groupthink: Psychological studies of policy decisions and fiascoes* (2nd ed.). Boston, MA: Houghton Mifflin.

Karnazes, D. (2005). *Ultra marathon man.* New York, NY: Penguin Books.

Kessler, R. (2000). *The soul of education.* Alexandria, VA: ASCD.

Khalili, O. (2009). *Why Pangea Organics founder Joshua Onysko thinks "sustainability" is for slackers.* Retrieved from http://causecapitalism.com/pangea-organics

Kushner, H. S. (2001). *Living a life that matters.* New York, NY: Alfred A. Knopf.

Loehr, J., & Schwartz, T. (2003). *The power of full engagement.* New York, NY: Free Press.

Lyubomirsky, S., King, L., & Diener, E. (2005). Review of research challenges assumption that success makes people happy: Happiness may lead to success via positive emotions. *Psychological Bulletin, 131*(6), 803–855. Retrieved from http://www.apa.org/news/press/releases/2005/12/success.aspx

Marketdata Enterprises. (2010). *The U.S. market for self-improvement products and services.* Retrieved from http://www.marketdataenterprises.com/pressreleases/SIMkt2010PR.pdf

Nichols, M. P. (2009). *The lost art of listening.* New York, NY: Guilford Press.

Orloff, J. (2009). *Emotional freedom.* New York, NY: Harmony Books.

Plessinger, A. (n.d.). *The effects of mental imagery on athletic performance.* Retrieved from http://www.vanderbilt.edu/ans/psychology/health_psychology/mentalimagery.html

Porter, K., & Foster, J. (1990). *Visual athletics.* Dubuque, IA: Wm. C. Brown.

Rana, S. (2005). *Stepping into possibility thinking.* Retrieved from http://www.articlesbase.com/management-articles/stepping-into-possibility-thinking-1835.html

Reiss, K. (2007). *Leadership coaching for educators.* Thousand Oaks, CA: Corwin.

Robbins, J. (1987). *Diet for a new America.* Tiburon, CA: H. J. Kramer.

Rock, D. (2006). *A brain-based approach to coaching.* Retrieved from http://www.resultscoaches.com/files/CoachingTheBrainIJCO.pdf

Rogers, E. M. (2003). *Diffusion of innovations.* New York, NY: Free Press.

Ross, J. (2000). *The diet cure.* New York, NY: Penguin Books.

Rubenstein, J., Meyer, D., & Evans, J. (2001). Multitasking undermines our efficiency. *Monitor on Psychology, 32*(9), 13.

Schwartz, J. M., & Begley, S. (2002). *The mind and the brain.* New York, NY: Regan Books.

Seligman, M. (2002). *Authentic happiness.* New York, NY: Free Press.

Sisson, M. (2009, July). *Creative visualization.* Retrieved from http://www.marksdailyapple.com/creative-visualization-urban-legend

Smith, C. (2009). *What's coaching when it's at work.* Retrieved from http:www
.coachingknowhow.com/whats-coaching-when-its-at-work/

Spira, J. B. (2005, September). *The cost of not paying attention.* Retrieved from
http://www.basex.com/web/tbghome.nsf/23e5e39594c064ee852564ae
004fa010/ea4eae828bd411be8525742f0006cde3/$FILE/CostOfNot
PayingAttention.BasexReport.pdf

Stone, H., & Stone, S. (1993). *Embracing your inner critic.* New York, NY:
HarperCollins.

Tenberken, S. (n.d.). *Climbing blind: Tibet expedition.* Retrieved from http://
www.touchthetop.com/gallery/album.php?Climbing-Blind-Tibet-
Expedition-7

Thabet, D. (n.d.). *Smile 400 times a day.* Retrieved from http://www.articlesbase
.com/motivational-articles/smile-400-times-a-day-3713850.html

Tolle, E. (2006). *A new earth.* New York, NY: Penguin Press.

Trungpa, C. (2010). *Smile at fear.* Boston, MA: Shambala.

United Press International. (2007). *Future focused CEOs bring innovation.*
Retrieved from http://www.upi.com/Business_News/2007/08/15/
Future-focused-CEOs-bring-innovation/UPI-20741187208809/

Veenhoven, R. (n.d.). *World database of happiness.* Retrieved from http://
worlddatabaseofhappiness.eur.nl

Waitley, D. (1995). *The psychology of winning.* Niles, IL: Nightingale-Conant.

Wheatley, M. J. (1998). *The promise and paradox of community.* Retrieved from
http://www.margaretwheatley.com/articles/paradox.html

Wheatley, M. J. (2007). *Finding our way.* San Francisco, CA: Berrett-Koehler.

Wilder, M. (1983). *Break my stride.* New York, NY: Kobalt Music.

Zilbergeld, B., & Lazarus, A. (2008). *Liu Chi Kung was imprisoned for seven
years during the Cultural Revolution.* Retrieved from http://iaoj.wordpress
.com/2008/06/02/liu-chi-kung-was-imprisoned-for-seven-years-
during-the-cultural-revolution

Index

CORWIN

A SAGE Company

The Corwin logo—a raven striding across an open book—represents the union of courage and learning. Corwin is committed to improving education for all learners by publishing books and other professional development resources for those serving the field of PreK–12 education. By providing practical, hands-on materials, Corwin continues to carry out the promise of its motto: **"Helping Educators Do Their Work Better."**